# Free from the Sea

LANNICE SNYMAN and ANNE KLARIE

# Free from the Sea

The South African Seafood Cookbook

*A complete alphabetical guide to the identification and preparation of South African fish, shellfish and molluscs, with 159 tried and tested recipes to help you make the most of the food that we can still get free . . . from the sea.*

**Don Nelson, Cape Town**

*First edition 1979*
*Second impression 1980*
*Third impression 1981*
*Printed by Citadel Press, Lansdowne, Cape*

ISBN 0 909238 38 3

PHOTOGRAPHS by Jac de Villiers
STYLING by Lin Sampson
ILLUSTRATIONS by Anne Klarie
SEAFOOD for the photographs prepared by Lannice Snyman
assisted by Annette Barratt

*To our husbands Michael and Peter for baiting our hooks,
removing wriggling fish therefrom and for their
indulgence in our culinary experiments.*

# Contents

## Colour Plates (in order of appearance)

*recipe number*

# Metric Conversion

The measurements used in this book are in the form of metric cups, tablespoons (Tblsp) and teaspoons (tsp).

## Volume

| | | | | | |
|---|---|---|---|---|---|
| 1 Cup | 250 mℓ | $\frac{1}{3}$ Cup | 80 mℓ | 1 tsp | 5 mℓ |
| $\frac{3}{4}$ Cup | 190 mℓ | $\frac{1}{4}$ Cup | 60 mℓ | $\frac{1}{2}$ tsp | 3 mℓ |
| $\frac{1}{2}$ Cup | 125 mℓ | 1 Tblsp | 12,5 mℓ | $\frac{1}{4}$ tsp | 1,5 mℓ |

## Oven Temperatures

| | Very cool | Cool | Moderate | Moderately hot | Hot | Very hot |
|---|---|---|---|---|---|---|
| °C | 110 | 140 | 160 | 190 | 220 | 240 |
| | 120 | 150 | 180 | 200 | 230 | |
| °F | 225 | 275 | 325 | 375 | 425 | 475 |
| | 250 | 300 | 350 | 400 | 450 | |
| Gas Mark | $\frac{1}{4}$ | 1 | 3 | 5 | 7 | 9 |
| | $\frac{1}{2}$ | 2 | 4 | 6 | 8 | |

## Weight

| Metric | Approximate Imperial Conversion | Metric | Approximate Imperial Conversion |
|---|---|---|---|
| 1 Kilogram | 2,2 lb | 150 grams | 5 oz |
| 900 grams | 2 lb | 100 grams | 4 oz |
| 750 grams | 1 lb 10 oz | 75 grams | 3 oz |
| 500 grams | 1 lb 2 oz | 50 grams | 2 oz |
| 250 grams | 9 oz | 25 grams | 1 oz |
| 200 grams | 7 oz | | |

## Liquids

| Metric | Approximate Imperial Conversion | Metric | Approximate Imperial Conversion |
|---|---|---|---|
| 1 litre | 35 fl. oz | 125 mℓ | 4 fl. oz |
| 250 mℓ | 9 fl. oz | 75 mℓ | 3 fl. oz |
| 200 mℓ | 7 fl. oz | 50 mℓ | 2 fl. oz |
| 150 mℓ | 5 fl. oz | 25 mℓ | 1 fl. oz |

# Acknowledgements

We are indebted to many people for their encouragement and assistance during the compiling of this book. In particular . . .

Jac de Villiers for his magnificent photographs and Lin Sampson for her expert and imaginative styling. Their enthusiasm made each session sheer joy.

Ralph Krall and Babsie van Zyl for kindly allowing us to invade their homes with our cameras and fish.

Mrs Margaret Smith of the J. L. B. Smith Institute of Ichthyology, Rhodes University, Grahamstown for her interest and assistance.

Marika Bowes for sharing with us her vast knowledge of seafood.

I & J for information and some of the seafood required in our test kitchen.

The Fisheries Development Corporation of South Africa Limited, for the oysters for our photographs.

Kloof Nek Road Fish Market, Cape Town, for providing their most perfect fish for the photographs.

Lynette Barling for her assistance with editing and proof reading.

Johann Snyman, who taught his family the ways of fish and fishing.

Don Nelson, our Publisher, for his infinite wisdom and patience.

## BIBLIOGRAPHY

SMITH'S SEA FISHES
  by Prof. J. L. B. Smith (Valiant Publishers)

SEA AND SHORE DANGERS
  by Margaret M. Smith

NEW LAROUSSE GASTRONOMIQUE
  by Prosper Montagné

SALT WATER FISH AND FISHING IN SOUTH AFRICA
  by K. T. Lilliecrona

PICTORIAL GUIDE TO S.A. FISHES
  by K. H. Barnard

THE MASTER CHEFS. A HISTORY OF HAUTE CUISINE
  by E. B. Page and P. W. Kingsford (Edward Arnold)

# Introduction

This book is a culmination of many pleasurable hours spent together both at the seaside and in our kitchens experimenting with, and learning more about the delicious art of preparing seafood.

Our kitchens have been many and varied – from the comfort of our own homes to the primitive kitchens we've shared along much of our coast-line, where necessity has truly been the mother of invention. Our experiments have resulted in many a tasty dish using beach-rubbed rocks to tenderise tough perlemoen, crushed corn flakes to coat freshly-caught fish, and using a leafy twig as a basting brush for crayfish sizzling over open coals.

Our book has been divided into three sections: the first deals with Selection, Preparation, Methods of Freezing and Methods of Cooking seafood.

The Second is an Alphabetical Index of each type of seafood relevant to this book. Each section includes common names, a line drawing to help identify your catch, interesting information about it, what we consider the most successful cooking methods and a list of recipes.

Compiling this index has taken many hours of painstaking research. South Africans have a habit of endowing their fish with different names in each part of the country and this has caused many headaches for naturalists and anglers – as well as ourselves!

There have been occasional attempts to standardise these names, all of which have come to naught. Happily so, for the quaintly descriptive nicknames will remain part of our heritage. Haarders, for instance, will always be referred to as mullet or springer, and our musselcrackers will always be known by their seventeen different common names.

We are greatly indebted to Professor J. L. B. Smith. His *Smith's Sea Fishes* has been a constant companion during our months of research. We would also like to acknowledge helpful correspondence from his widow, Mrs Margaret Smith.

Thirdly, there is the Recipe Section: you'll notice that we've devised many original recipes as well as adapted classical dishes to accommodate our local seafoods. All have been thoroughly tested, with the help of our long-suffering husbands and friends. That they proffered their platters for 'seconds' is proof of our success.

The enjoyment of seafood is rather like the enjoyment of wine – everyone has his or her own particular favourites. So too in the preparation of seafood: we have cross-referred many types of seafood and fish which can be substituted in each recipe, taking into account texture, flavour and size. We do, however, urge the imaginative cook to experiment even further, only by experimenting will seafood cooking become for you what it has for us – constantly challenging, always fulfilling and most rewarding.

# Seafood and Poisoning

Common sense and the sea go hand in hand. The dangers of the sea and sealife must be understood and respected by all those who enjoy the pleasures of our shores.

Mrs Margaret Smith of the J. L. B. Smith Institute of Ichthyology at Rhodes University, Grahamstown, has published a book entitled *Sea and Shore Dangers* which covers everything from sunburn to shark attacks and is a must for anyone who ventures to the sea, whether it be to sail, swim, dive, fish or simply to walk along its beaches.

Some people are allergic to seafood and should never eat it. Those unfortunate enough to have this allergy soon know about it as the symptoms are occasionally unpleasant enough to make a tracheotomy necessary in severe cases. If your ears start itching within an hour of eating seafood, make that your last seafood meal; the allergy worsens every time you indulge.

For the rest of us there is still a danger of poisoning, unless the following rules are obeyed:

1. Never eat blaasop or sunfish.
2. Never eat mussels, oysters or clams from areas infected by a toxic red tide.
3. Never eat the liver or roe of the red steenbras, kob, wreckfish or shark. The high vitamin A content may cause poisoning.
4. Collect mussels, oysters and sea urchins at low tide when you can get as far away as possible from the danger of pollution from the shore. Avoid any seafood from polluted areas like harbours and near sewage or factory waste pipes.
5. Make sure your seafood is fresh or has been properly stored and frozen. Poisoned fish has a sharp peppery flavour.

# Selection, Preparation and Methods of Freezing

Follow your nose – that's the best method of ascertaining whether seafood is absolutely fresh. Freshness is vitally important in all seafood cookery.

Ideally, all seafood should be cooked within a few hours of being caught, but as this is not always possible, freezing is the next best thing.

The South African Fishing Industry brings high quality frozen seafood into all parts of the country, enabling everyone to enjoy it even if geography denies one the pleasure of catching one's own. Whether one requires prawns for two or five kilograms of fish specially 'shatterpacked', it is readily available. The bulk packs give one the economy of buying in bulk and the thrift of removing as much fish as required without any wastage.

It follows too, that freshly-caught seafood is also the best for freezing, as seafood from your fishmonger or supermarket has probably already been frozen and thawed. Never forget – all seafood must be scrupulously cleaned and well wrapped to be successfully frozen. It will then keep for up to six months.

A great deal has been written about the brightness of a fish's eye, the redness of its gills and the firmness of its flesh, so nothing more need be said on the subject. Every cook by now should be able to recognise a fresh fish at a glance. If you're about to store fish for a few days in the fridge, clean, wash well, dry and cover it.

## BLEEDING
This improves the flavour of the flesh of some fish, and must be done as soon as the fish is caught. Cut the gills and let the blood flow freely in a pool of water.

## SCALING
Hold fish by the tail and, with the blunt edge of a knife, scrape away scales with swift movements from tail to head. If you have difficulty in scaling, plunge fish in boiling water for a few moments, rinse well, then proceed. Scales may then be removed in a trice.

## CLEANING
Slit fish along belly, remove entrails and rinse clean. Clip off gills with a sharp pair of scissors or a knife. When cooking fish whole, leave on head and tail. If you're going to stuff the fish, remove entrails from the neck.

*Flatfish*, like sole, have their entrails in a cavity behind the head. Slit behind head, clip off fins and clean as above.

## SKINNING

*Fish with insignificant scales:* Make an incision with knife tip at head. Grip skin with dry cloth and pull off skin quickly with one deft movement. Rinse in cold running water.

*Fish with scales:* After cleaning, scaling and filleting, place skin-down on board. Pin skin down with a fork then using a sharp, flexible knife, press firmly down and away from fork and cut skin away from flesh.

*Sole* is skinned from tail to head. Lay fish, dark side up, on board and make a slit just above tail. Hold tail and pull skin off towards head. Remove white skin the same way.

## FILLETING

With a sharp knife, slice carefully down length of backbone and cut fillets free on either side.

## FREEZING

After thoroughly cleaning and drying, fish can be frozen whole – stuffed or as is – in cutlets, fillets, minced (for use in fish cakes) or crumbed. Wrap securely and label clearly before freezing.

*NOTE: Specific preparation of Shellfish and Molluscs are treated in their sections.*

# Cooking Methods

Despite the wealth of fine fresh fish and shellfish available in our country, seafood cookery is probably the least understood and most frequently abused form of cookery in our homes and restaurants. Yet it is not difficult to become an expert.

In order to avoid loss of flavour and succulence, seafood should always be cooked for a minimum amount of time at as low a heat as possible. This rule also applies to frying and barbecuing, when a moderate heat is preferable.

Do remember – you're dealing with exquisite and delicate flavours, so when following recipes, don't take too many liberties with the herbs and spices indicated. Rather use less than risk overpowering the flavour of the dish with too heavy a hand.

### FRYING

Always stand over your frypan to ensure perfect timing, and never fry over too high a heat. Frying slowly ensures moist, tender results. It is impossible to give timing estimates, as your heat and the thickness of the fish must be taken into account. As a guide, fish fillets 3–4 cms thick should take 2 minutes on each side. Another way to time fried fish is to watch until the fillet becomes opaque half-way up, then flip over to complete the cooking process.

Various coatings can be used when frying seafood:

Seasoned flour, or milk and flour. (Fish will brown better if you dip it in milk before flouring.)

Flour, egg and breadcrumbs. (Adding ground almonds will make a delicious difference.)

Batter, [Recipe No's 4, 5 and 6]

Or simply season firm fish and fry till golden brown in hot butter and garlic. Heat butter until you see it browning, then quickly add chopped garlic and your fish. Reduce heat at once to fry at a more moderate temperature to avoid the butter burning.

## GRILLING

Brush both fish and grid with oil before grilling to prevent sticking, and allow grill to become piping hot before cooking. Score the skin of the fish beforehand to prevent the fish from twisting and, after browning, season with salt, pepper and lemon juice. We need hardly remind you that left-over juices make a delicious sauce.

As a timing guide, grill fish 3 cms thick for 3–4 minutes on each side.

An exotic variation on the theme of grilling fish, is to sprinkle it lightly with a mixture of rosemary, fennel, parsley and thyme, pour over 2 Tblsp warmed brandy and ignite. The burning herbs will give the fish an irresistible flavour.

Marinate your fish for an hour or two before grilling, using marinades and basting sauces [Recipe No's 29, 30 and 31].

## BAKING

Baking is considered best for dryer types of fish which can be baked whole, stuffed, in cutlets or fillets. The latter two take far less cooking time, depending, of course, on size and thickness of your fish.

Add a minimum of liquid as fish, while it is cooking, forms its own juice. For a special touch, add cream to the baking liquor and use as a separate sauce.

Various combinations of ingredients such as onions, tomatoes, mushrooms, garlic, bacon, wine and herbs can be added to make baked fish more interesting.

*Baking in foil* is quick, easy and most successful. It seals in the natural flavour and keeps fish succulent. Season fish, dot with butter and seal in well oiled foil. No liquid need be added, though one could sprinkle a few drops of lemon juice or dry white wine over the fish before sealing.

Serve a separate sauce with your baked fish. See recipes 7 to 23.

## STEAMING

One is inclined to associate steamed fish with invalid cooking and consequently imagine the resultant dish will be dull and insipid, but this need not be so. With intelligent use of herbs, seasoning and sauces, steaming can bring out the most delicate fish flavours, without loss of moisture. The liquid produced by the steaming process should always be retained and added to your sauce.

Instead of adding herbs, try steaming fish between layers of well-washed seaweed. See how the flavour of the sea comes through.

Serve the steamed fish hot or cold with a complementary sauce.

## POACHING

It is always more desirable to poach fish in court bouillon (recipe 1) than in either water, or water with onions and seasoning, as the flavour of the court bouillon is developed before the fish is added. The dish will then be twice as tasty.

Always poach *very* slowly; the liquid should barely move. Your fish is cooked as soon as it becomes opaque. It can then be drained if it is to be eaten hot, or cooled in the poaching liquid before skin and bones are removed.

A teaspoonful or so of either vinegar or lemon juice keeps the flesh of fish snowy white and firm.

## BRAISING

Unlike poaching, braising uses far less liquid in the cooking process and as a result less flavour is lost. Again may we stress: don't waste the resultant ambrosial liquid – it is a valuable addition to your sauce or fish stock.

Place fish in an ovenproof dish, season with salt, freshly-ground black or white pepper, herbs and finely sliced onion. Add either a little fish stock and white wine, or stock and water, cover tightly, basting occasionally while cooking.

## ROASTING

Roasting is best for firm, dry types of fish like tuna. Cook either plain or stuffed fish in oil.

Pour 3 cms of oil into roasting pan and heat in oven till piping hot. Dust fish with seasoned flour and brown quickly all over, taking care not to break the skin when turning. Reduce heat to 180°C and cook, uncovered, for approximately 30 minutes per kilo.

The secret of successful roasting is to baste fish frequently to keep the flesh from drying out and to ensure an all-over crispness.

# BARBECUING

Most fish and many shellfish may be cooked over an open fire, though naturally some are more successful than others.

Seafood barbecues can add a new dimension to your entertaining and enhance your enjoyment of seafood. They can be as simple or elaborate as you like, from cooking a single, freshly-caught fish over a beach fire, to presenting a tempting selection of different types of fish and shellfish served with marinades, sauces and tasty accompaniments.

All fish are even more delicious cooked on a solid plate or plough disc, on which butter, garlic and herbs have been placed. Substitute a few layers of foil, if you have no disc. This keeps the flesh moist and succulent and prevents delicate-fleshed fish from falling apart. It also provides a tasty sauce with which to serve the fish.

The most delicate-fleshed fish are best barbecued in buttered foil, and whole fish cooked in this way can be stuffed. After cooking, fish may be removed from the foil and carefully browned over the coals to capture the inestimable barbecue flavour.

Nothing quite tops the flavour of firm-fleshed fish barbecued over the coals. Using a hinged grid solves the problem of the flesh breaking up as one turns it. Place the tail-end of the fish towards the hinge so you can further regulate the pressure of the grid on the flesh.

To repeat – do liberally oil both fish and grid before cooking to prevent sticking.

An aromatic addition to barbecued fish is to sprinkle either fresh fennel, dill or thyme, or dried mixed herbs on the glowing coals at the end of the cooking process.

Rock-feeders like blacktail, elf, galjoen etc. are much fatter in the winter months, when storms have churned up the water and provided them with food. This is why they're 'vlekked' by cutting down past the backbone and hinging open at the stomach, before being cleaned and prepared for the grid. Season with pepper only before cooking and with salt to taste afterwards. Salt has the effect of drawing the juices from the fish and drying out the flesh.

Cook skin-side down first. This will allow the fat in the flesh to be cooked in, and makes a great difference to the finished dish. Fish cooks surprisingly quickly, especially over open coals. Keep a moderate heat; never cook fish too quickly and don't overcook it.

## BARBECUING TIPS

We list below those fish and shellfish which can be barbecued most successfully, with a few hints to help you become an expert 'Fish Braaier'.

ALIKREUKELS          See recipe 41.
ANGEL FISH           Very firm-fleshed. Fillet and barbecue on grid. Marinate and baste frequently.

†Numbers refer to recipes in the section commencing on page 79

17

| | |
|---|---|
| BARRACUDA | Dry flesh. Marinate, baste and don't overcook. |
| BLACKTAIL | Flesh breaks easily. 'Vlek' and barbecue on disc or in a hinged grid, skin side down first. Season with pepper before cooking and with salt to taste afterwards. |
| BREAM | See Blacktail. |
| BLUE HOTTENTOT | See Blacktail. |
| CAPE SALMON | Firm-fleshed and fairly dry. Marinate and baste. Remove skin before serving. |
| DAGERAAD | 'Vlek' and barbecue on disc or in hinged grid. Baste frequently. |
| ELF | See Blacktail. |
| GALJOEN | Barbecue the fattest fish caught in the winter months. 'Vlek', leaving skin and scales intact and the head and tail in situ. Season with pepper before barbecuing, skin side down first, and salt to taste afterwards. |
| GRUNTER | The only way to destroy the flavour is to burn it! 'Vlek' and cook as for Galjoen. |
| HAARDER | Fillet down backbone. Salt and dry for about 4 hours. Barbecue on grid. |
| JOHN BROWN | Firm fleshed and tough-skinned. Barbecue as Galjoen and remove skin before serving. |
| JOHN DORY | See Dageraad. |
| KABELJOU | See Cape Salmon. |
| LANGOUSTINE | Barbecue on steel plate or disc with plenty of garlic butter, or on grid. |
| LEERVIS | See Barracuda. |
| LIMPETS | Shell down, cook as is or brushed with butter. |
| MACKEREL | See Haarder. |
| MARLIN | Very dry. Marinate, baste frequently and don't overcook. |
| MUSSELCRACKER | See Blacktail, or barbecue in foil, then crisp over open coals after cooking. |
| MUSSELS | See recipes 73 and 74. |
| PERLEMOEN | See Alikreukels, recipe 41. |
| PRAWNS | See Langoustine. |
| ROCK LOBSTER | See recipe 110. |
| SILVER FISH | See Musselcracker. |
| SNOEK | Fillet and barbecue on grid. Don't overcook, as it becomes very dry. Baste frequently. |
| SWORDFISH | See Marlin. |
| TUNA | See Marlin, or recipes 152, 153 and 154. |
| WHITE STEENBRAS | See Blacktail. |
| ZEBRA | See Blacktail. |

# SMOKING AND CURING

These methods were evolved before the time of refrigeration and fast transport and are still popular today.

## HOT SMOKING

Home-smoking apparatus is easily obtainable and it is both quick and economical to smoke many types of firm-fleshed fish successfully. The metal box is 35 cms by 55 cms and 3 kilos of fish can be smoked to perfection in 15 minutes. Oak sawdust or oak shavings are the best to use – get them from your hardware store.

For perfect results with your home-smoking, salt fish heavily with coarse cooking salt. Leave for 2 hours. Wash off salt, hang fish out to dry for 12–24 hours, then smoke.

## COLD SMOKING

This is done in a drum, using smoke only and no heat to cure the fish. This method is utilised commercially for a wider market.

## SMOKED FISH

Smoked fish makes interesting hors d'oeuvres, sandwich fillings, snacks, dips and of course, in the many interesting recipes in this book which call for it.

## CURING/SALTING

After cleaning the fish, fillet through past backbone leaving the two fillets hinged together. Season heavily with coarse salt and hang to dry where there is plenty of air circulation. For a perfect salt balance, wash the salt off after one hour and re-salt lightly. Leave to dry again until the skin becomes taut, sealing in the soft flesh.

*NOTE: Smoking and Curing are, in fact, methods of half-cooking, so don't expect it to keep for longer than a week. After that fish can, of course, be wrapped and frozen.*

# Seafood A–Z

# Alikreukels

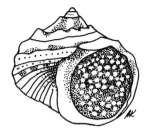

Tough but very tasy, alikreukels are considered a great delicacy by lovers of shellfish.

Cook in boiling salted water, in their shells. As soon as their 'trap door' comes off easily (after 15–20 minutes), they're cooked. Remove fish from shell and remove 'trap door' and stomach, and use in any of the suggested recipes.

# Angel Fish

Sliced in half on plate 1

BATFISH/SEABAT

48 cm*

Young angel fish are yellow or orange, patterned with crossbars, and the colour and bars fade as they grow to dusky adulthood. When startled, the young wrinkle up their fins and sink slowly to give the appearance of a dead leaf.

Angel fish steaks are tasty, dry and very firm, and are most successful when they're:

+ Fried
+ Baked and served with a sauce
+ Barbecued or Grilled
+ Smoked

†Numbers refer to recipes in
  the sections commencing on
  page 19

* Throughout the book these figures refer to average lengths.

# Baardman

BELVIS/TASSELFISH

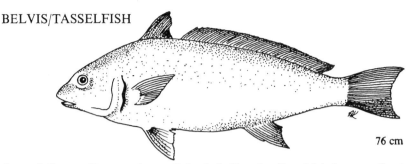

76 cm

RECIPES

*Wine-Baked Stumpnose,
145*

*Mushroom and Almond
Bream, 45*

*Smoked Fish Recipes,
see p. 19*

One of the smaller members of the kabeljou family which has excellent flesh. The soft-bodied young, however, are unmarketable and are given an unprintable name by the trawler hands.

Baardman is scrumptious:

* Fried
* Poached

* Baked
* Smoked

# Barbel

BARBEL-EEL

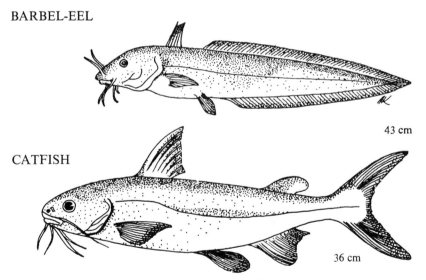

43 cm

CATFISH

36 cm

The barbel's ugliness belies its piquancy. When properly prepared the flesh of the barbel-eel particularly, is one of the tastiest in our seas – in the same class as sole, so next time you catch a barbel, don't throw it back into the sea – you'll be missing out on a treat.

At Imperial Roman banquets where those partaking ate their '. . . broths with spoons of amber', they served with their seafood courses 'the beards of barbels instead of salades, mix'd with oil'd mushrooms'.

23

Muddy brown in colour, with elongated, scaleless bodies and serrated spines, these fish can cause painful lacerations and even death to the handler. Do be extra careful when handling the live fish.

Barbels are best:

* Fried
* Grilled

# Barracuda

SNOEK/SEAPIKE

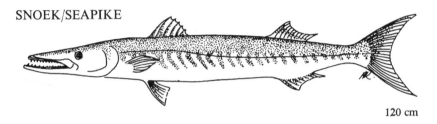

120 cm

Said to be the most ferocious of all creatures, they kill simply for the fun of it. As they reach a massive 1,8 m, they may well command the greatest respect! The flesh, however, is most delicate, and when exquisitely prepared and cooked makes a memorable repast.

* Braai
* Grill
* Fry
* Smoke

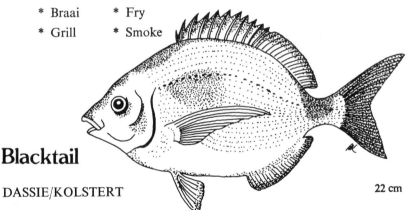

# Blacktail

DASSIE/KOLSTERT                    22 cm

A small but vigorous angling fish unique to the African coastline. The young have fine bars which change as they grow, to become almost black in adulthood, with their characteristic darker spot above the tail.

They are excellent eating but, like many fish, become tougher and coarser as they grow older – like most of us – more's the pity.

There's nothing nicer than *fresh* blacktail filleted, skinned and . . .

* Deep fried
* Baked
* Barbecued
* Lightly salted and heavily smoked

24

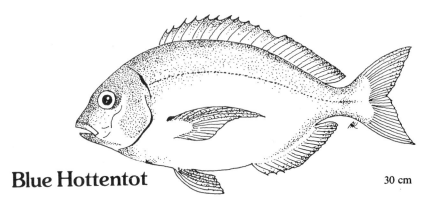

# Blue Hottentot

30 cm

BUTTERFISH/DAS/JOHN BROWN (JANBRUIN)/FATFISH (VET-VIS)
BLUEFISH/BUTTER BREAM/BRONZE BREAM/COPPER BREAM/
DAMKOKKER

These beautiful, plump fish have firm, white flesh, and their average weight is 1–2,5 kg. Strangely enough, you'll occasionally come across a tough, almost rubbery specimen, but they're still very good eating, most tasty . . .

    * Fried        * Grilled

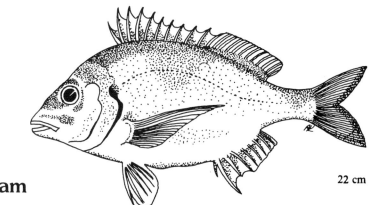

# Bream

22 cm

MUD BREAM/SLY BREAM/PICNIC BREAM/RIVER BREAM/
BLACK BREAM/RIVER PERCH

One of South Africa's well-known angling fish; it has excellent flesh. It is known by many different names due to its variable form and colour and is one of our favourite food fishes, prepared in almost any manner, but most popular . . .

    * Fried        * Poached
    * Grilled or Barbecued

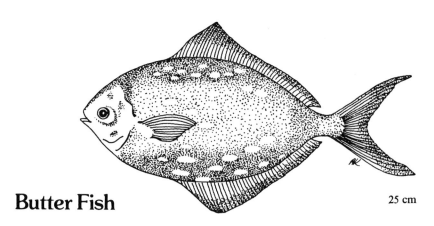

25 cm

# Butter Fish

CAPE LADY/PAMPELMOES/BLUEFISH (BLOUVIS)

A beautiful small fish with luscious, delicate flesh which does not keep well, not that it ever has to – it's so toothsome a dish! As soon as possible after it is coaxed from the deep, your butter fish is best . . .

* Fried

# Cape Salmon

SALMON/GEELBEK

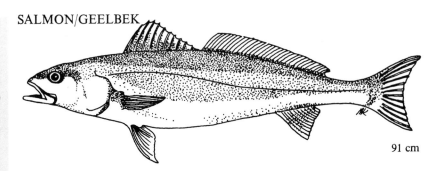

91 cm

This highly-esteemed fish is easily distinguishable by the bright yellow colour inside the mouth. The flesh of this fish is superior to that of the more common kabeljou – a second cousin.

Cape Salmon is easy to cure and this has resulted in our unique Cape delicacy, 'Geelbek Toutjies', [47].

* Poach in court bouillon and serve with a sauce
* Fry in garlic butter, or with a coating of batter
* Bake (smaller ones, up to 2 kg)
* Pickle
* Cure
* Grill or Barbecue

# Crab

See plates 1 & 3

These shellfish are highly prized throughout the world and their flesh is similar to that of rock lobster, though a trifle more delicate. The flavour of fresh crab is quite different to that of tinned crab, something to bear in mind when preparing the more delicately-flavoured fresh meat. Though it's a fiddly and time-consuming task it is worthwhile taking the trouble to prepare the small sand crab which are reasonably plentiful.

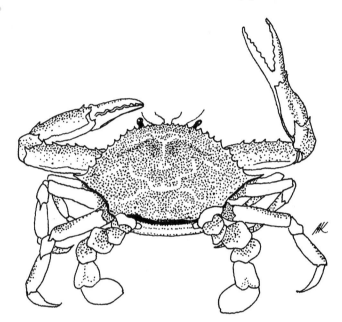

## PREPARATION

Suffocate fresh crabs by immersing them in fresh water for a few hours before cooking, as live crabs have a tendency to lose their legs and claws when plunged straight into boiling water – a sorry state of affairs for all concerned!

Plunge the late lamented crabs into heavily salted boiling water (at least 2 tablespoonfuls per 4 litres of water), return to the boil, cover and simmer for 10 minutes only. Remove from the water and allow to drain right side up.

To extract flesh, remove abdomen flap and prise off upper shell. Remove the gills from either side, and the intestines. Rinse lightly, break into halves and remove flesh from each segment and from the claws.

*RECIPES*

Crabs can be frozen whole if so desired (well wrapped in plastic) or the flesh stored in small containers to save freezer space. When required for use, thaw slowly and drain.

Frozen crabs may be stored for up to six months.

Enjoy fresh crab with lemon juice or vinegar and plenty of freshly-ground black pepper, or in a salad with seafood sauce.

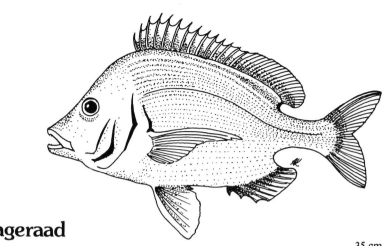

# Dageraad

35 cm

REDFISH/DAGGERHEAD/SLINGER

As their souls leave their bodies, waves of the most incredibly beautiful colours of an early-morning sky pass over their skin and scales, hence the name 'Dageraad' – dawn. A delectable small fish.

* Fry
* Bake and serve with a sauce
* Grill or Barbecue, basting continuously

# Eel

Edible eels in our waters include: EEL (PALANG)/CONGER EEL/ MORAY EEL/CONGER PIKE/SILVER CONGER and SAND-SNAKES (SLANGETJIES)

These tasty fish are not as popular in South Africa as in other parts of the world, but considering their appearance, one can imagine why – they're just not pretty!

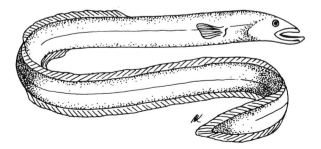

They're found in all rivers flowing from east to west into the sea, as well as in the sea. As a general guide, larger eels tend to be a bit coarse and oily.

Prof J. L. B. Smith suggests a simple method of trapping sand-dwelling eels: dig bits of smelly fish along the edge of the surf at low tide. This will entice the eels from their sandy homes and they can then be speared. Sounds like good fun for a summer evening!

PREPARATION

Beware! All eels are dangerous and they're not easy to kill. Give the fish a hard blow on the back of the head and make sure it's quite dead before proceeding!

Skin by slitting around neck, cutting off tail and, gripping the head, pull skin off towards tail. Sprinkle fish with salt and leave for a few hours. Cut off head, slice fish open, remove entrails and clean well. Trim fins, lay fish on it's back, slit through to backbone and remove bone carefully.

* Fry, with a coating, and serve with a sauce
* Stuff and Bake
* Poach and serve with a sauce
* Smoke

# Elf

SHAD/SKIPJACK/TAILER

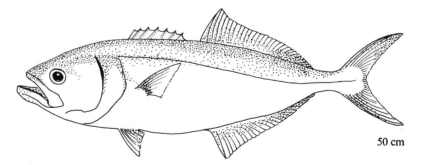

50 cm

A vicious fighter and one of our best-known angling fishes, with excellent flesh, delicately flavoured and moist. It spoils quickly, however, so cook as soon as possible after it stops wriggling.

* Fry
* Grill or Barbecue
* Smoke

29

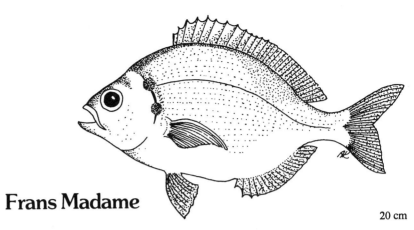

# Frans Madame

20 cm

JACOBEVER/DIKOOG/PEULOOG/GROOTOGIE

A member of the bream family and as the name implies, a most attractive small fish. The flesh is tasty, but its diminutive size limits it to being cooked whole.

* Fry          * Bake

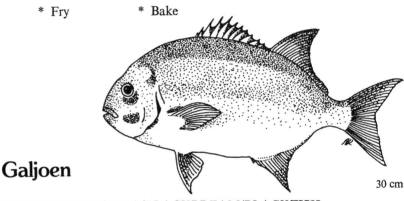

# Galjoen

30 cm

HIGHWATER/DAMBA/BLACKBREAM/BLACKFISH

Aptly named after that stately Spanish sailing vessel – the galleon – and unique to South African waters. The galjoen is affectionately considered our national fish by anglers.

They feed very close inshore and for this reason are at their fattest and juicy best during the winter months when storms have churned up the sea – and morsels of food. Fish caught in summer are scrawny and hardly worth eating.

The unusual flavour and marbled, black-veined flesh of a corpulent Galjoen is a fish you either love or hate. It is usually bled in a rock pool after being caught to improve the flavour and is traditionally served with its head and tail in situ.

* Grill or Barbecue     * Bake
* Fry

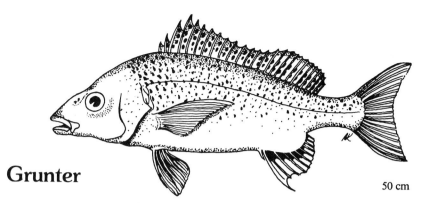

# Grunter

50 cm

SILVER GRUNTER/BULL OR COCK GRUNTER/KNOORHAAN/
TIGER/SPOTTED GRUNTER

So named, because when it comes from the water, spasms of the throat muscles cause the teeth to rasp together, which sounds like a man – not a gentleman – clearing his throat!

The larger of the species are excellent eating and are best . . .

* Barbecued
* Fried

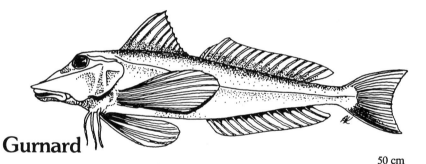

# Gurnard

50 cm

KNOORHAAN

Quaint-looking with its large head encased in a bony shield. It grunts or croaks when taken from the water. Well, wouldn't you if you happened to be a gurnard?

The nickname 'Poor Man's Sole' describes gurnard best, and it can be used as a substitute for the more expensive sole. It is firm-fleshed and well-flavoured.

To clean, simply slit open, bend the head backwards, give a tug and pull the skin off. The fillets can then be cut off the bone.

* Fry, with a coating
* Poach whole, then fillet and serve with a well-flavoured sauce
* Wrap in bacon and grill

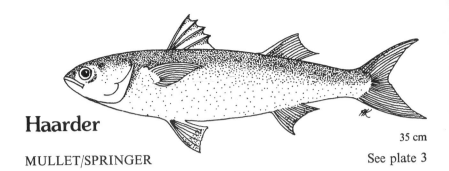

# Haarder

MULTLET/SPRINGER

35 cm

See plate 3

One of our most important food fishes, being firm-fleshed and well-flavoured, though rather on the small side and very bony. They have great leaping powers, hence the nickname 'Springer'.

Haarder can be prepared in many different ways.

* Filleted, dipped in egg and breadcrumbs and fried for $1\frac{1}{2}$–2 minutes on each side
* Freshly-caught, rolled in brown paper and baked
* Poached
* Soused
* Smoked (one of the nicest fish to smoke)
* Salted with coarse salt and dried ('Bokkems'), rather like Geelbek Toutjies [47]
* Barbecued, after salting and drying for a few hours

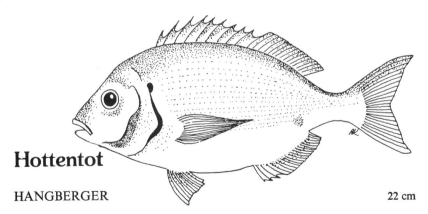

# Hottentot

HANGBERGER

22 cm

These dusty-faced fish have a most distinctive flavour – not to everyone's liking. Their flesh is not very firm and remains moist even during grilling and smoking. The smaller fish are very bony.

We have enjoyed it most . . .

* Poached in strong court bouillon
* Well-seasoned and baked, in both cases it must be served with a tasty sauce.

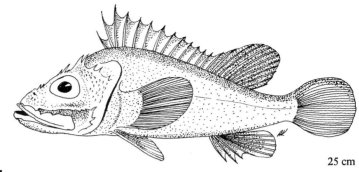

25 cm

# Jacobever

SANCORD

An attractive red fish with delicately-flavoured flesh, marketed in South Africa as Sea Bream. It reaches a length of about 35 cms, and is most popular . . .

* Fried

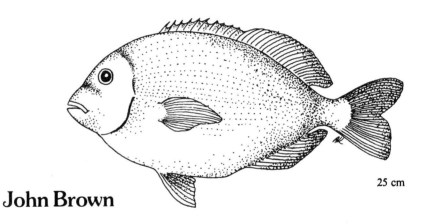

25 cm

# John Brown

JANBRUIN/BLUE-EYE JOHN BROWN/BLAUWOOG JANBRUIN

This plump shapely fish is typically South African, and distinctive with its dark brown body, bright blue eyes and large, comical teeth. One of our tastiest rock fishes regretably becoming less and less abundant.

The flesh is very firm, almost tough, and should be skinned if it's to be fried or grilled.

* Skin, fry in butter and olive oil. Add a squeeze of lemon juice to the butter sauce and serve separately.
* Grill or Barbecue, basting continually
* Smoke

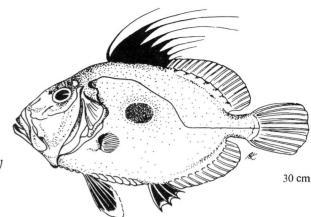

# John Dory

GIRTIE

Nicknamed 'St Peter's Fish' because the young have a dark spot on each side, said to have been the marks left by St Peter's thumb and forefinger as he picked it up.

John dory is a raggedy-looking creature, but the flesh is delicately-flavoured, rather like trout. It is traditionally grilled or barbecued over glowing coals, always with herbs and basting sauce to enhance the flavour. The head is considered a great delicacy, so it is usually left in situ.

* Season well, coat with egg and flour or breadcrumbs and fry in butter and oil
* Poach and serve with a sauce          * Grill or Barbecue
* Bake                                   * Braise

30 cm

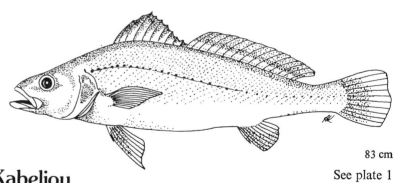

83 cm

See plate 1

# Kabeljou

KOB/SALMON/SALMON BASS/RIETBUL/BOERKABELJOU

One of our most important and versatile food-fishes, with all but the largest having delicate, tasty flesh. Kabeljou have been known to reach 1,8 m in length.

* Fry          * Pickle
* Poach        * Bake
* Smoke        * Grill or Barbecue

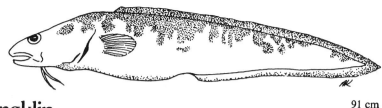

91 cm

# Kingklip

Quite unmistakable with its elongated body and mottled pink colouring, kingklip is in great demand as a table fish. The liver is considered a great delicacy. Like kabeljou, they are known to reach 1,8 m in length, but average much less.

* Fry – this is the most popular way of preparing Kingklip
* Poach
* Bake
* Grill

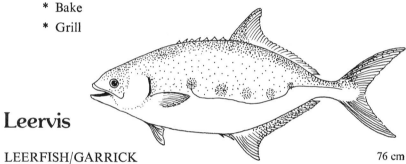

# Leervis

LEERFISH/GARRICK                                    76 cm

No doubt about it, leervis is the best game fish in our seas, eagerly hunted by anglers.
  The smaller fish are good eating, but the flesh becomes coarser and dryer as they get bigger, when they are best skinned and pickled or smoked.

* Fry in butter, or butter and oil, and serve with lemon-butter sauce
* Bake in foil, to retain moisture
* Barbecue        * pickle

# Limpet   See plate 3

BARNACLE

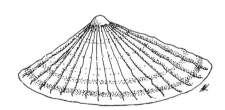

The midden heaps of prehistoric strandlopers show that they lived largely on limpets and mussels.
  The midden heaps of the future will show that people of the twentieth century also enjoyed these molluscs – though served in a slightly more sophisticated manner.

Steam limpets out of their shells in a little water, and enjoy with garlic butter or french dressing, the liquid mopped up with chunks of healthful crusty whole wheat bread. Nothing could be nicer.

Limpets may also be eaten raw, or brushed with butter and grilled or barbecued in their shells.

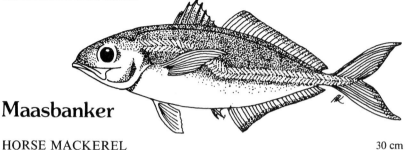

# Maasbanker

HORSE MACKEREL                                                          30 cm

Small, bony fish with a strip of sharp, prickly scales down each side which must be cut out. The flesh is dark, rich and tasty, and is invaluable to our canning industry.

* Smoking and Curing are, perhaps, the best methods of preparation
* Fry
* Souse
* Barbecue

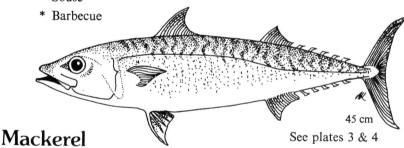

# Mackerel

45 cm
See plates 3 & 4

One of the smallest members of the tuna family, which *must* be eaten fresh. Try not to handle it too much, and don't leave it in the sun. Cut the red meat away along the sensory line.

* Pan fry in oil and butter
* Grill or Barbecue – a particularly good method of preparation, as the flesh is oily and the skin is thick.
* Poach and serve with a sauce
* Poach, then sprinkle with fresh, chopped herbs and lemon juice and pop it in the oven for a few minutes to grill
* Souse
* Smoke
* Pickle

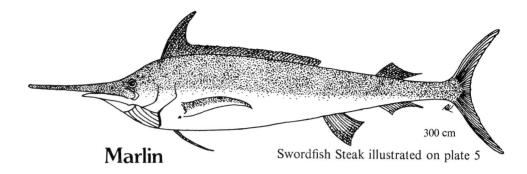

300 cm

## Marlin

Swordfish Steak illustrated on plate 5

SPEARFISH and SWORDFISH/BROADBILL

Only in South African waters are all four species of the marlin found: the black, the blue, the striped and the white. Not only are they eagerly sought by anglers for sport, but marlin steaks are something quite special.

The famous and pugnacious swordfish, cousin of the marlin, is rarely caught, but its flesh is just as highly esteemed.

Marlin and swordfish flesh cannot be compared, flavour-wise, with anything else, although in texture they are similar to tuna.

The time-honoured method of grilling marlin steaks cannot be improved upon. Season with salt, pepper, aromat and a squeeze of lemon juice. Grill quickly and serve immediately. Do *not* overcook – the fish will dry out.

* Grill or Barbecue
* Smoke

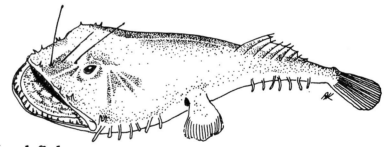

## Monkfish

91 cm

ANGLERFISH

A rather odious-looking fish which is rapidly gaining popularity in South Africa due to its firm, tasty flesh. It is considered a great delicacy in Japan, and is often used as a substitute for rock lobster, though it is **not as** flavoursome.

* Poach in court bouillon and serve with a tasty sauce
* Fry

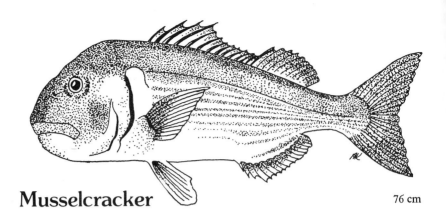

# Musselcracker

76 cm

You're forgiven for being confused about what a Musselcracker really is – there are two types in our waters, which between them, have seventeen common names!

SAND STOMPKOP/SANDBLOUER/MUSSEL CRUSHER/STEEN-
   BRAS/SILVER STEENBRAS/BRUSHER, and the second type:
BISKOP/BLACK BISKOP/BLUE BISKOP/POENSKOP/STOMPKOP/
   BLOUER/BANKBLOUER/WITBEK/STEMBRAS/STEENBRAS/
   BLACK STEENBRAS

Both types develop characteristically large heads and powerful jaws, and are considered fine angling fish.

Younger fish are good eating, but the flesh coarsens with age. The head is considered a delicacy. Firm, white musselcracker steaks are most successful:

* Fried
* Poached
* Smoked
* Pickled
* Baked
* Barbecued in foil, then crisped on a steel plate

# Mussels and Clams

See plates 1 & 3

Black, brown and white mussels are among our most tasty molluscs. There is no such thing as a 'safe season' for collecting and eating them but, being molluscs, they take in water from the sea around them as well as anything in the water, like bacteria, which is then condensed in their systems. If these substances are poisonous, such as bacteria from a sewerage system, or from a toxic red tide, the mussels themselves will be poisonous to eat and will remain so until the water is cleansed and the molluscs themselves have had a chance to cleanse their systems.

It follows, therefore, that a few simple rules apply to safe mussel-eating. Never collect mussels from areas which may be polluted, because of, for example, their proximity to sewage and factory waste pipes or harbours. In tidal zones, collect mussels from the deepest areas, where they are further from the influence of shore pollution. Most important of all, watch for the red tide. It isn't always toxic, but rather be safe than sorry.

Discard any whose shells are broken or cracked or which remain open after you've tapped the shell. They should close smartly. Cook within a few hours of collecting.

Clams of American clambake and chowder fame, are quite different to Mussels in appearance. Their shells are almost circular, smooth and white in colour, some exquisitely criss-crossed with beige and brown stripes.

Sometimes confused with scallops or white mussels, clams have a flavour and texture all their own; slightly firmer than Mussels and to some, tastier.

In preparation, clams are treated exactly the same way as mussels, although in some parts of the world they're eaten raw, like oysters.

## TO PREPARE

Scrape shells clean, rinse under running water, then leave in a bucket of fresh, cold water for half an hour. During this time they will 'spit out' any sand which they may have inside.

## TO COOK

Fill a large saucepan half-way up with cleaned mussels. Add just enough water to cover the bottom of the pan. Cover, bring to the boil and steam the mussels open. As soon as they open, they're cooked, so remove them immediately with a pair of tongs. Discard any that remain shut.

When cool enough to handle, remove one or both shells, depending on how you wish to serve them, and carefully pull out the beard. Ensure they're free of sand by once again rinsing in cold running water. Strain the stock from the saucepan for use in your sauce or soup, or freeze it for later use.

## TO FREEZE

Steam mussels open as above, remove completely from their shells and freeze in strained stock. Don't attempt to freeze dry as they rapidly lose flavour and texture. Remember too, to remove them from the saucepan the moment their shells open, as overcooked mussels don't keep well.

Mussels are among our most versatile seafoods, and can be prepared in a variety of ways. There is nothing more delicious though, than freshly-steamed, hot mussels, dipped in french dressing or garlic butter.

When eating mussels from their shells, *never* use a fork – pluck them out with another mussel shell; they're ready-hinged for the job.

# Octopus

SEACAT

There is one method of preparing this oddity of the sea which has stood the test of time; it was probably devised by the ancient Greeks and is used even today by epicures.

When one has enticed the multi-legged creature from its rocky home with a red-flagged stick, murder it gently with a whack against a suitable rock. Continue bashing until it's tenderised, skinless and quite, quite dead, pausing between every ten bashes to scour it all over against the rock until it foams. Stop before there's a danger of it disintegrating.

Remove the mouth, turn the head inside out and wash well.

Alternatively, if you're against making a spectacle of yourself on the beach, hang your octopus up on a nail, skin it with a sharp knife then beat the tentacles with a mallet to tenderise the flesh.

Place the now-tender octopus in a dry saucepan over a medium heat, cover and cook gently in its own juices. It will turn red and soon become tender; test with a fork to know when it's cooked. 10–15 minutes should be sufficient.

One may now . . .

* Cut it up and fry, without coating. Serve with a squeeze of lemon.
* Make into biltong by cutting into strips, seasoning with salt and pepper and wind-drying for a few days.
* Make into one of the lush dishes mentioned above.

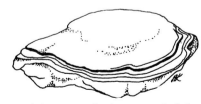

# Oysters    See plates 1, 3 & 7

Oysters should be eaten kneeling – honest! Anyone who has sampled the delicious flavour of a fresh, raw oyster should offer thanks to the ancient Romans who originated the art of eating them. These marvellous molluscs are considered a delicacy practically all over the world.

To cater for the demand, oyster farms have become big businesses and oystermen are getting so skilful that, by draining the beds once a day and depriving the mature oysters of water, they teach them to keep their mouths shut when they're out of water. This, plus skilful packing, allows us to enjoy fresh oysters far from the sea. Another advantage is that cultivated oysters contain a higher percentage of meat than a coast oyster of a similar size.

It is essential that oysters are kept chilled to ensure they're still alive when eaten fresh out of their shells. Refrigerated, they'll remain perfectly fresh for up to 7 days and in cold winter weather may be quite safely stored unrefrigerated for up to 3 days. It's a simple matter to check for freshness – the two shells must be tight shut, or should close when tapped.

Prise the shell open at the hinged end with an oyster knife, if you have one, being careful to avoid spilling the liquid. Serve as is, with lemon wedges, cayenne pepper, brown bread and butter and a glass of stout.

Cooked oysters are often served in the deep half of their shells. To keep them upright, settle them in a layer of coarse salt on the baking tray before filling and grilling them.

# Periwinkel   See plate 3

WINKLE

In appearance and flavour these shellfish are like miniature Alikreukels. They are eaten raw in many parts of the world, but we prefer them cooked.

Soak freshly-gathered winkles in fresh water for half an hour, rinse well under running water and drain. Poach for five minutes in boiling, salted water, timed from when water starts to boil. Drain, cool, and remove winkles from their shells with a pin. With your fingers, pull off the protective disc and soft stomach, rinse again and enjoy as is or with Garlic Butter or French Dressing. (Recipes 8 and 9)

Prepare periwinkles as above for use in any of the suggested recipes.

# Perlemoen   See plates 1 & 3

ABALONE/KLIPKOUS

Elsewhere in the world, perlemoen is known as 'Ormer', a corruption of the French 'oreille de mer' or 'sea ear'.

41

We cannot understand why it is not more popular than it is; it's a most delicious and very adaptable shellfish.

In our experience, pressure cooking is quite unnecessary, but steaks *must* be beaten to make them tender, and should never be overcooked as they become tough. Thinly sliced steaks dipped in egg and breadcrumbs or batter take only one minute to fry.

### PREPARATION

Remove the fish from the shell while it's still alive. Whack it on the 'mouth' with a blunt but lethal weapon, such as a stone or a hobnailed boot. This will stun the fish and make it more amenable to being cut out of its shell. Scrub off the black slime, using a hard brush or pot-scourer, trim off the skirt, cut out the mouth and your perlemoen is ready for cooking or freezing.

To prepare for cooking, slice into steaks, then beat carefully and thoroughly with a mallet, keeping thumbs out of the way. One can feel when the flesh is tender.

### FREEZING

We prefer freezing perlemoen whole after they've been cleaned and trimmed. This way it's much easier slicing into steaks while they are semi-frozen, using a knife or a bread slicer.

Perlemoen may be kept frozen much longer than other seafood. We have used it successfully after 12 months in the freezer, finding it even more tender after that time, though it does lose some of its flavour. If you do keep it frozen for many months, use the flesh in a more strongly-flavoured recipe like Perlemoen Peperonata or Perlemoen Parmigiani.

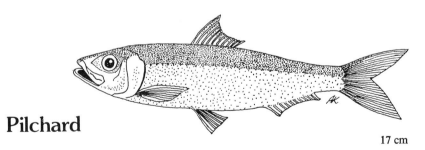

# Pilchard

17 cm

## HERRING/SARDINE/WHITEBAIT/ANCHOVY

All members of the same family. They're grouped together as they're all similarly prepared.

Although on the small side and rather bony, these fish are extremely versatile and are of considerable value commercially. Think of kipper, rollmops and pickled herrings, and the extent to which these fish are tinned, smoked and salted.

We've read somewhere that the word 'herrings' comes from the Teutonic word 'heer' meaning an army. This aptly describes the shoals in which these fish usually travel – shoals so densely packed that larger fish dare not enter for fear of being suffocated.

The tiniest fish of the family are best pickled, soused or dipped in flour and deep fried, and served as snacks or entrées. The gourmet would never dream of topping or tailing them, but would eat them whole – using a fork only. That's etiquette, I believe.

Larger fish may be baked, grilled, or fried – coated with flour, seasoned oatmeal or semolina – and served as a main course.

Kippers are traditionally grilled, with a knob of butter placed on the fleshy side, boiled in a bag or poached.

All members of the pilchard family can be . . .

* Fried
* Grilled
* Baked
* Smoked
* Pickled
* Soused

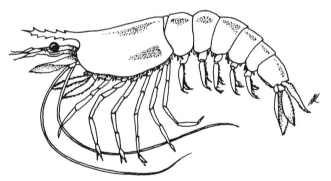

See plates 1, 3 & 5

# Prawns, Shrimps and Langoustine

For the purpose of this book, these shellfish have been grouped together, as they are similar in appearance and texture, varying of course, in size.

They're usually purchased either fresh or frozen (in blocks of water) or all nice and hygienic – and soulless – in tins. Like crab, the tinned variety differs in flavour when compared with the fresh or frozen variety.

## TO PREPARE FRESH PRAWNS, SHRIMPS AND LANGOUSTINE

If they're to be used in their shell, first remove the vein down the back. Slit the shell, then pull the vein out carefully. Langoustine, being larger than prawns, are usually cut in half anyway, and the vein can then be easily removed. We usually remove the head as well and discard it.

To remove shell, pull off the head, slit shell along underside between legs, then bend off – using your thumbs – towards the back. The shell and tail can then be easily removed. De-vein by straightening the fish, then pulling out the vein carefully, from the head end. If it refuses to budge, or breaks off, make a small incision along the back and then remove. Rinse and pat dry.

## TO COOK

For use in salads or cocktails, remove shell, de-vein, rinse clean, then drop into boiling salted water. See that they cook for one minute only, from the time the water comes to the boil a second time. Overcook at your peril – they become powdery and are fit only for the compost heap.

Besides being boiled as above, prawns and langoustine are delicious . . .

* Grilled
* Fried
* Barbecued

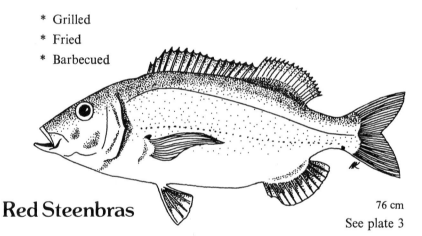

## Red Steenbras

76 cm
See plate 3

YELLOW STEENBRAS/STEENBRAS

A fine angling and table fish; one of the few whose flesh hardly coarsens with age. (Some creatures have all the luck.)

A few words of warning, though – large and irritable specimens have been known to turn nasty and attack divers. Their powerful jaws studded with large teeth can cause serious injuries.

*Never eat steenbras liver* – it is poisonous. The high vitamin A content causes loss of skin and body hair, as does the liver of a braised Polar Bear, though you'll probably never be tempted to try bear in any shape or form.

Red steenbras is best . . .

* Baked, preferably stuffed.
* Barbecued, but be sure to marinate and baste it.

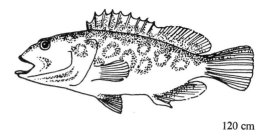

# Rock Cod

120 cm

GARRUPA/YELLOWBELLY/BLACK SEABASS/LANTERN FISH
BUTTERFISH/BLACKFISH
BLACK BESS/WRECKFISH/STONEBASS
SPOTTED ROCK COD/KINGKLIP (KONINGKLIP)

There are 10 species of rock cod in our seas and these denizens of the deep can grow to a massive 450 kg.

They are among our most important food fishes, though their tasty flesh must be skinned.

* Frying is the preferred method of cooking rock cod.

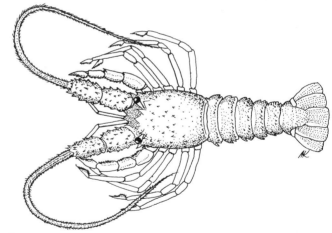

# Rock Lobster

See plates 1 & 3

CRAYFISH/LOBSTER

If you're not lucky enough to have caught your own, test for freshness by stretching out the tail. It should flip back smartly or else . . .

TO PREPARE

It is kinder to drown Rock Lobster in fresh water before cooking. Cook to perfection by weighing it beforehand, placing it in a large saucepan of

45

hot water or court bouillon – using enough liquid to cover it completely. Boil for 6 minutes per 500 g, and start timing when liquid starts to boil again. The flesh can now be easily removed from legs, body and tail.

To remove raw flesh from tail, cut along both sides where the softer underside shell meets the back shell. Peel off underside shell, lift out meat and remove and discard the alimentary canal.

## FREEZING

The flavour is better preserved by freezing rock lobster raw, although flesh in the body and legs may have to be sacrificed as it becomes too difficult to remove. What we prefer to do is to freeze raw tails separately, washed, dried and packed in airtight freezing bags, and to cook the bodies for immediate use, or for storing in the freezer in small quantities. Shells may be removed from tails before freezing or after thawing.

To freeze cooked lobster, boil as described above, drain well, resting right side up, leave until cold then pack very well in airtight freezing bags, with their tails curled tightly into their bodies.

Raw rock lobster keeps for up to six months in the freezer. To test if it's been in the freezer too long, crack off a leg. It should not be hollow or dried out. Cooked flesh has a shorter life-span, becoming powdery and dry after 2-3 months.

To defrost raw or cooked rock lobster, place on kitchen paper which will absorb the excess water. Thaw *slowly*.

Psychologically, one of the secrets of all tempting food is this: It must give its consumer trouble – not make things too easy for him; that is why a cold lobster should never be separated from its shell except by he who eats it. Garnished, of course, with vinegar or Seafood Sauce!

# Roe

Roe is the spawn of the fish; when cooked it has a delightful texture and with careful seasoning can be prepared in many interesting ways. All too often this delectable substance is discarded when the fish is cleaned.

A word of warning: Poisoning can result from eating the roe or liver of several species of fish which have a high vitamin A content, or as a result of fish being in contact with pollution from the land. Play safe and don't eat the liver or roe of the red steenbras, kob, wreckfish or shark, or of any species which is unfamiliar or which has been in contact with polluted water.

Caviare is the roe of the sturgeon and calls to mind an interesting custom relative to this royal fish. Whenever it was caught in England, on the Wye or elsewhere, a portion of the fish was offered to the King.

Extracting the roe of the sturgeon requires skill acquired only through experience. Immediately the fish is caught it is bled and gutted and the eggs are carefully removed. They are then placed on a special sieve to be washed, drained and salted.

The Sturgeon, like many other species of fish, is becoming more and more rare so Russian scientists have developed an operation which allows the fish to be returned to its watery home after the removal of the roe. No wonder caviare is so costly! Only the true gourmet eats it as it should be enjoyed, that is – a goodly portion, as is with only a sprinkling of lemon juice to enhance the flavour. Lesser mortals like you and I must be content with an occasional smattering on our canapés.

When faced with the roe of a fresh fish, here's what to do: Wash clean under running water then simmer intact for 5 minutes in water to which you've added 1 tsp vinegar. Drain, cool, split it in two, season with salt and pepper and fry the cut side in hot butter for a minute or two. Serve with lemon wedges.

Alternatively, remove and discard the skin of the simmered roe, cut roe in slices and add to a fish salad or use in one of the recipes listed above.

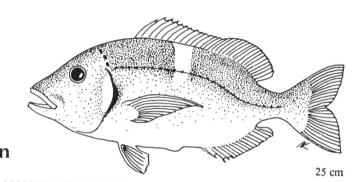

# Roman

RED ROMAN/DAGGERHEAD

25 cm

See plates 1 & 3

A beautiful, bright orange fish, with choice flesh. When large enough, it is particularly delicious stuffed and baked (specimens over 1,5 kg are rare); the flesh is firm and the flavour is strong.

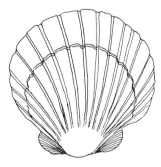

# Scallop

A Scallop is a delicacy in the luxury class – in a word a Ritzy seafood – fresh or frozen.

TO PREPARE

Wash and scrub the shells then place scallops, rounded side up, on a baking tray in a hot over. As soon as the top shell shows signs of rising, lift off with a knife. Remove flesh, trim away beard and black intestinal thread. Wash flesh and the little coral tongue, then drain and dry. They're now ready for use.

Place white flesh and coral in a saucepan of cold water, bring to the boil, remove scum and simmer for 3–4 minutes. Or simply season with salt, white pepper and a pinch of cayenne pepper, dip in batter or crumbs, deep fry and serve with a sauce.

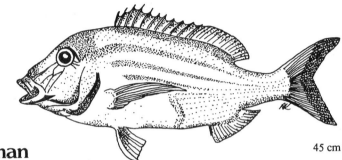

45 cm

# Scotsman

Although not plentiful, this deepwater Caledonian is excellent eating, especially . . .

* Fried and served with a sauce

# Sea Urchins     See plate 3

Fanciers of these spiky delicacies comb the rock pools at low tide armed with a sharp pair of scissors and lemons, to enjoy their dozen while they're at their freshest. Gourmet urchin-eaters will be recognised by the fact that they carry cayenne pepper, brown bread and butter – and a bottle of cold white wine as well!

Sea urchins are seasonable – best collected at Spring Tide and beneath full moon. The deeper under the water they live the better (less likelihood of contamination from the land), and they *must* be fresh. Don't refrigerate them or leave them in the sun. There is a freshness test, though, if you're not going to eat them on the rocks: Sprinkle salt into the hollow mouth – if they start moving, they're safe to eat.

Pruning gloves make the opening operation easier. Cut right round the shell and discard the top. Turn urchin upside down, rinse quickly in sea-water, and you'll see the edible portion inside – bright red and with the appearance of caviare. (The female is brighter in colour than the male.) Season with lemon juice and cayenne pepper and eat raw. The flavour is most delicate and one to two dozen make a complete, healthy meal.

If you find the inside is mushy and black, don't eat it – you're out of season!

Besides eating them raw, sea urchins can also be lightly boiled. They were prepared by the ancient Greeks who, of course, taught the Romans their culinary skills, by wrapping them in fig leaves and placing them in the ashes of the fire to cook.

RECIPE

*Boiled Sea Urchins, 125*

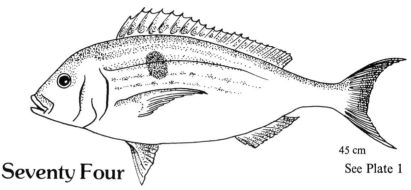

# Seventy Four

45 cm

See Plate 1

RECIPES

*Angel Fish Niçoise, 43*
*Mushroom and Almond*
*Bream, 45*
*John Dory Meunière, 58*

This elegant fish was at one time abundant but has become scarce in recent years. It got its name from lines on its body resembling rows of gun ports of an old "Seventy-Four".

Its highly esteemed flesh is most delicious . . .

\* Fried and served with a sauce.

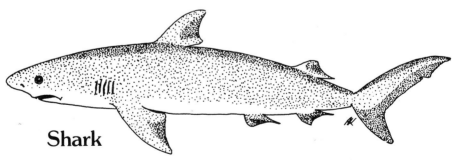

# Shark

The flesh of smaller sharks is tender and toothsome – simply melting in the mouth – rather like that of skate. In many parts of the world shark is highly valued as food and it is interesting to note that shark-hunting is directly linked with a reduction in shark attacks on bathers and skindivers.

Edible sharks in our waters include:
ST. JOSEPH SHARK, SANDSHARK, SAWSHARK, MILKSHARK, YOUNG GREY SHARK, RAGGED TOOTH (also called YELLOW or

BROWN SHARK), SPINY DOG FISH (also called PIKED DOGFISH, DOGFISH, SPIKY JACK or PEN HAAI – but be careful of his spines!), TIGER SHARK (also called SKAAMHAAI or SKAAMOOG)
Shark steaks are marketed in South Africa under the name 'Flake'.

When your shark is landed, kill and bleed it by cutting the gills and hanging it by the tail. Once ashore, skin and fillet it, taking steaks from the tail section. Lay the steaks in seawater or salted fresh water. After 20 minutes or so a frothy substance will apear on the surface of the water. Change the water three or four times until no more froth appears. Your shark will now be free of the odour of ammonia and you may proceed to prepare them in any of the ways listed below.

* Dip in egg and flour and fry
* Bake
* Mince and make into fishcakes
* Poach and serve with a sauce
* Make into shark biltong, following the method for Geelbek Toutjies [47].

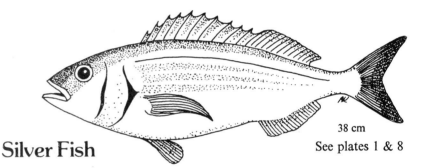

38 cm
See plates 1 & 8

## Silver Fish

DOPPIE/ROOITJIE/KARP/KARPENTER or KAAPENAAR

Silver fish are pretty fish with fairly firm, strongly-flavoured moist flesh. Tinier specimens usually end up in fish cakes, stock or fish soup, but the larger of the species are delectable . . .

* Fried          * Baked

# Skate

RAY

Not very strongly flavoured, so skate is best served with a complementary sauce. It has a faint odour of ammonia which disappears during cooking.

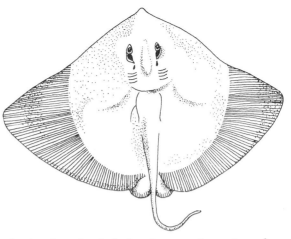

For ten hours after having been landed, the skate continues to re-form a sticky coating over its skin, so by wiping it, you'll soon see whether this coating re-forms and whether or not it's fresh.

*Only use* the fins, but ask your fishmonger to skin them for you; this is no easy task. Skate steaks are best . . .

  * Poached in court bouillon   * Fried

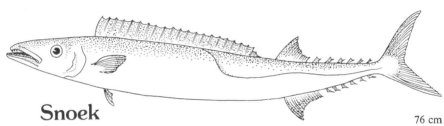

# Snoek

76 cm

The bite of the snoek is feared, as it has razor sharp teeth and fishermen swear that there is something present in the mouth which prevents the blood clotting in the wound it inflicts on the careless handler. We believe though, that it is the serrations on the teeth which cause jagged lacerations and consequently profuse bleeding.

They're important game fish with tasty flesh though some people find it a trifle oily.

The flesh of fresh snoek should be tinged with pink, and the fish firm; overhandling and the rays of the moon falling on the fish cause the flesh to go soft and spoil the fish for cooking.

Here's a tip that the Cape Coloured folk have used for years: Soak filleted snoek in salted, luke-warm water for several hours. The oil will separate from the flesh and float to the surface. Dry fish well and . . .

  * Fry, without coating

  * Grill   * Smoke (undoubtedly the best fish to smoke)

  * Barbecue  * Pickle

51

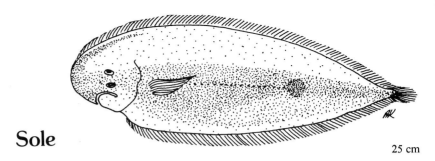

## Sole

25 cm

TONG/FLOUNDER/FLATFISH                    See plates 1 & 3

Found in most seas and characterised by the fact that the eyes lie on one side of the head, either right or left, and that the two sides usually differ in colour, the underside light, the upper darker and variable.

Sole is highly-prized as a table fish, its delicately-flavoured flesh is very versatile, but rather expensive. It can be cooked whole or filleted. See p 14. for preparation.

Simple, classical dishes are best suited to bring out the flavour.

* Fry
* Grill, brushing first with melted butter, or marinate first in oil and lemon juice.

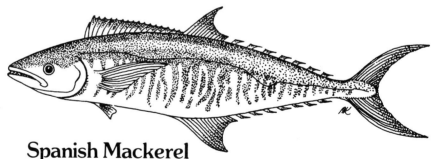

## Spanish Mackerel

100 cm

BARRACUDA/KATONKEL/NATAL SNOEK/WAHOO

Members of the large tuna family, these exicting game-fish have rich, tasty flesh.

* Fry without coating
* Grill
* Barbecue
* Smoke
* Pickle

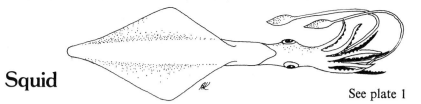

# Squid

See plate 1

CHOKKA/CUTTLEFISH/INK FISH. Also called 'CALAMARI'

Another of our delicious seafoods that is sorely underrated. We've prepared it in many different ways, each more tasty than the last.

## PREPARATION

Grasp the tail and head sections firmly in your hands and pull them apart. Lift the ink sac from inside the tail section and set aside. With a sharp knife cut tentacles free, just beyond eyes. Discard entrails and eyes.

With your fingers, remove the small round cartilage from the core of the tentacles' base and pull the tail skeleton out. Discard this cartilage. Pull fins away from tail cone. Remove fine membrane from fins, tail cone and tentacles. Wash everything and dry thoroughly.

## FREEZING

Clean and dry well as described above, then pack in airtight freezer bags or wrap.

Prepare squid for the table by steaming for 3–5 minutes to tenderise, then . . .

* Frying in garlic butter and serve on a bed of rice
* Deep frying in hot oil, with a coating. Remember that overcooked squid is tough and leathery.

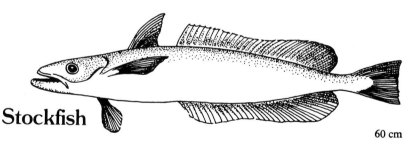

60 cm

# Stockfish

HAKE/HADDOCK/COD

Our most important commercial fish and our most popular table fish, being fairly firm, delicately-flavoured and comparatively inexpensive.

* Poach, and serve with a tasty sauce
* Fry, with some form of coating
* Grill
* Bake
* Smoke

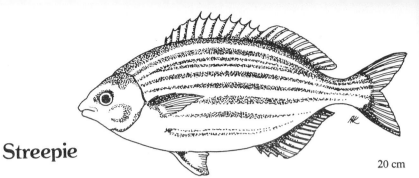

# Streepie

20 cm

BAMBOO/MOOI NOOITJIE/KARANTEEN

Most streepies are too small to rate as important table fishes; they must be cooked very fresh, as the flesh rapidly softens.

Most anglers know this pretty fish well though, and, if not using it for bait, prepare it by . . .

* Frying
* Barbecuing
* Smoking

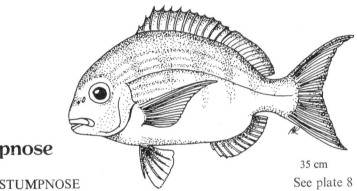

# Stumpnose

35 cm

WHITE STUMPNOSE

See plate 8

We have three closely-related fishes, all termed white stumpnose. All are brilliant silver, good eating and have the characteristic blunt head.

CAPE WHITE STUMPNOSE
BLINKVIS/SILVIE/FLATTIE/SILVER BREAM/BREAM
SILVER BREAM/YELLOW-FIN BREAM

RED STUMPNOSE

See plates 1 & 2

A frumpy looking fish, the adult males developing a big hump on the forehead as they grow older and wiser.

The flesh of the stump is strongly flavoured and is most delicious . . .

* Baked, plain or stuffed. Always cook it whole; the head is considered a delicacy.
* Grilled

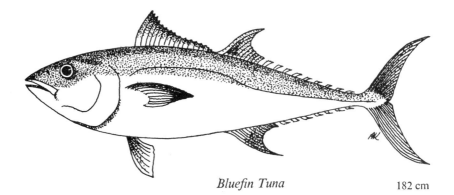

*Bluefin Tuna*                    182 cm

# Tuna

TUNNY

The large tuna family are commercially most important to South Africa. As a game fish it has brought considerable fame to the Cape, attracting sport fishermen from all over the world. We have more species of tuna in our waters than has any other country.

There's the big BLUEFIN, the thickset BIG EYE, the fighting YELLOWFIN and the LONGFIN or ALBACORE. Smaller members of the family are the TORPEDO TUNNY, the BONITO (called KATONKEL in the Cape), the MACKEREL (see separate entry) and the SKIPJACK which is mainly used for canning.

Canned tuna is an important stand-by in any pantry; it can be made up in many interesting ways, besides being used in cold buffets.

Tuna flesh is rich, tasty and inclined to be dry, so . . .

* Grill or barbecue, remembering to marinate and baste

* Roast

* Bake and serve with a sauce

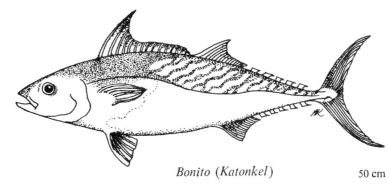

*Bonito (Katonkel)*                    50 cm

55

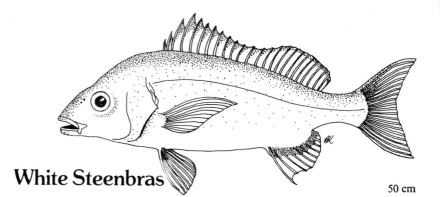

# White Steenbras

50 cm

WIT STEENBRAS/RIVER STEENBRAS/WHITE FISH/PIGNOSE
(VARKBEK)/GRUNTER
SAND STEENBRAS/SEABAS/BONTROK

These cousins are peculiar to South Africa and found all round our coast.
The sand steenbras is also called 'ghostfish' by skindivers because
it is difficult to see them under the water. Both are highly prized angling
fish, delicately flavoured, and the white flesh has large flakes when cooked.
Season well before . . .

* Grilling
* Frying
* Barbecuing
* Baking

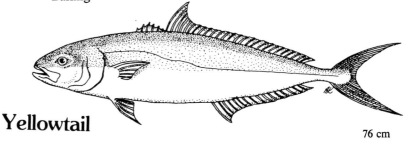

# Yellowtail

76 cm

ALBECORE

See plate 1

This fine game fish is brilliant blue with yellow fins, and sometimes has a
broad yellow stripe from head to tail below the blue. It is abundant in and
around False Bay in summer.

It's flesh is tasty, very firm, tends to be coarse and should be skinned.
Overcooking or cooking at too high a heat tends to make yellowtail dry.

It is best . . .

* Soaked for a few minutes in heavily salted milk, drained dipped
    in flour and fried in olive oil and butter.
* Grilled                * Pickled
* Barbecued              * Smoked

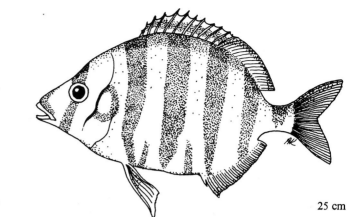

# Zebra

25 cm

WILDEPERD/BONTROK/STREEPDASSIE

Cousin to the blacktail, and an attactive and distinctive fish with its silvery-gold body and black bars. It is a rare and exciting fish to catch, giving a memorable fight. Anglers often speak of 'their' wildeperd as having been something special!

Zebra is one of our tastiest fish – considered superior to the blacktail – and can be prepared in similar ways:

* Lightly salted and heavily smoked
* Fried
* Barbecued – preferably in foil
* Baked

57

# Basic Recipes

# 1. Court Bouillon

2 cups water, or water and dry white
    wine
1 large onion, sliced
2 bay leaves
1 sprig parsley
    pinch thyme
1 tsp salt
½ tsp crushed black peppercorns

*For poaching 1 kg fish.*

Simmer, covered, for 30 minutes to allow the flavour to develop. Strain before adding fish.

# 2. Fish Stock

1 kg Fish trimmings (bones, heads, etc.)
1 sliced onion
2 sprigs parsley, or ½ tsp dried parsley
1 sprig thyme, or ⅛ tsp dried thyme
1 small bay leaf
1 tsp lemon juice
1 tsp salt
12 whole black peppercorns
3 cups water
1 cup dry white wine

*Many recipes call for the inclusion of fish stock, so always keep some on hand in your freezer. Get into the habit of making stock every time you have fish trimmings, or store the trimmings in your freezer until you have sufficient to make a brew.*

Simmer all ingredients gently together in a covered saucepan for 30 minutes. Strain.
    This recipe makes one litre of stock.

# 3. Quiche Pastry

2 cups flour
¼ tsp salt
1 tsp baking powder
150g cold butter
1 egg
3 tsp cooking oil
1 Tblsp water (or a little more, if necessary)

Sift together flour, salt and baking powder. Rub in butter lightly with fingertips. Combine egg, oil and water and add to flour mixture, to make a well-blended dough. Roll out and line a 25 cm pie plate. Prick the bottom with a fork.
    Chill for 20 minutes.

60

# 4. Basic Coating Batter

1 egg
½ cup milk
½ cup flour
¼ tsp salt

*Sufficient for 1 kg fish, 4 medium sized perlemoen or 6 medium-sized squid.*

Break egg into a bowl with half the milk. Mix well, then slowly stir in flour and salt, using a wooden spoon. Gradually stir in the rest of the milk to make a smooth batter about the consistency of honey.

# 5. Shantung Batter

1 egg
½ cup milk
½ cup flour
¼ tsp salt
⅛ tsp white pepper
½ tsp cumin
2 large cloves garlic, crushed
1 tsp hot English mustard
1 tsp French mustard

Mix egg and half the milk with a wooden spoon. Slowly stir in flour, salt, pepper and cumin. Add the rest of the milk, garlic and mustard. Blend thoroughly.

# 6. Bavarian Batter

340 ml (small bottle) beer
1 cup flour
1 tsp salt
½ tsp paprika

Sift together flour, salt and paprika. Slowly pour in beer, beating continuously with a wooden spoon until well blended.

# Sauces

# 7. Seafood Sauce

½ cup mayonnaise
½ cup cream (tinned cream is an excellent substitute in this recipe)
1 Tblsp tomato sauce
  salt and freshly-ground black pepper
  pinch cayenne pepper

*For use over any cold cooked, or canned fish or shellfish, in cocktails or with salads.*

Mix all ingredients together until smooth and creamy.

VARIATIONS ON THE SEAFOOD SAUCE

The possibilities of varying the basic Seafood Sauce recipe are endless. Add flaked fish, smoked fish, tinned tuna or salmon, cooked or tinned prawns, shrimps, oysters etc., chopped finely.

Serve on a bed of lettuce, in avocado pear halves, or use to stuff tomatoes.

Make the basic Seafood Sauce, omitting the cayenne pepper and tomato sauce, and try these pleasing variations:
  * 4-6 chopped anchovy fillets, 4 Tblsp chopped spring onions and one chopped hard-boiled egg.
  * One grated apple, sprinkled with the juice of half a lemon, ½ cup flaked, toasted almonds and ¼ tsp mixed herbs.
  * 1 tomato, peeled, seeded and finely chopped, 1 green pepper, even more finely chopped, 1 clove of garlic, crushed, ¼ tsp mixed herbs.
  * 1 tsp curry powder, 2 hard-boiled eggs, coarsely chopped, ¼ cup finely chopped nuts.
  * 3 Tblsp horseradish sauce, 2 Tblsp capers, ½ tsp sugar.

DIPS

Make all the above sauces into delicious dips by substituting 1 cup cream cheese for the mayonnaise.

# 8. Garlic Butter

Melt ½ cup butter in a small saucepan. When hot and frothy add 1–2 large cloves garlic, crushed or finely chopped. Sauté gently for a minute or two, being careful not to allow the butter to burn.

Serve with freshly cooked seafood.

# 9. French Dressing

1 Tblsp lemon juice
2 Tblsp vinegar
¼ tsp mustard (preferably Dijon)
  salt and freshly-ground black pepper
6 Tblsp olive oil, or half olive and half
    sald oil
  small clove garlic, crushed

*Delicious with steamed or barbecued mussels, prawns or over Salade Niçoise.*

Mix together lemon juice, vinegar, mustard, garlic and seasoning, then beat in oil until the dressing thickens, and emulsifies.

# 10. Mornay Sauce

2 Tblsp butter
2 heaped Tblsp flour
2 cups milk or milk and cream
  salt and freshly-ground black pepper
1 tsp English mustard
2 Tblsp dry sherry (optional)

*A memorable sauce to make any cooked fish, rock lobster or mussels a dish fit for the gods.*

Melt butter in small saucepan. Remove from heat and blend in flour, stirring until smooth, then add mustard and seasoning. Stir in ½ cup milk, blend well, then add remaining milk. Return to heat and cook until thick and smooth, stirring constantly. Remove from heat and stir in sherry.

# 11. Spicy Tomato Sauce

2 Tblsp chopped shallots or spring onions
1 Tblsp butter
1 tsp cornflour
¼ cup dry white wine or vinegar
1¼ cups ripe tomatoes, skinned and
    chopped (or tinned tomatoes)
1 Tblsp tomato paste
  salt and freshly-ground black pepper
  pinch cayenne pepper or a few drops
    tabasco
  pinch thyme or rosemary

Slake cornflour in wine.

Sauté shallots in butter until soft. Add tomatoes, tomato paste and seasoning. When it reaches simmering point, stir in cornflour and wine mixture slowly, stirring continuously.

Simmer for ten minutes or until the sauce is smooth and thickened.

# 12. Mushroom Sauce

1 Tblsp butter
1 cup fresh mushrooms, sliced
1 medium-sized onion, chopped
1 Tblsp cornflour
¾ cup water
¼ cup dry white wine
1 chicken stock cube
2 tsp soy sauce
　freshly-ground black pepper
　pinch thyme
⅓ cup cream
2 Tblsp parsley, chopped

*This subtly-flavoured sauce is especially delicious served with fish fried with a coating of breadcrumbs and ground almonds.*

Sauté onion and mushrooms in butter until tender. Slake cornflour in water and add to pan with wine and crumbled stock cube. Stir until sauce thickens. Add soy sauce, pepper and thyme. Reduce heat and simmer, uncovered, for 3 minutes. Add cream and parsley, stir and heat through.

# 13. Tartare Sauce

1 cup mayonnaise
1–2 tsp chopped parsley
1–2 tsp chopped tarragon
1–2 tsp chopped capers
　salt and freshly-ground black pepper

Mix ingredients together and serve with hot or cold fish or shellfish.

# 14. Green Mayonnaise

3 Tblsp chopped parsley
10 spinach leaves
1 cup mayonnaise
1 tsp crushed garlic
1 tsp lemon juice
　salt and freshly-ground black pepper

Boil spinach and parsley together in a little water for three minutes. Drain well, then blend all ingredients together in a liquidiser.

# 15. Sweet and Sour Sauce

2 Tblsp cooking oil
1 large clove garlic, finely chopped
1 green pepper, de-pipped and finely
    sliced
1 medium-sized carrot, finely sliced
½ medium-sized cucumber, peeled,
    depipped and finely sliced
½ cup chicken stock
4 Tblsp brown sugar
½ cup brown vinegar
2 tsp soy sauce
3 Tblsp tomato sauce
3 tsp cornflour slaked with ½ cup cold
    water

*Spoon over tasty, deep fried seafood and imagine you're at the Teahouse of the August Moon.*

Gently sauté garlic, green pepper, carrot and cucumber in oil for 2 minutes in a large frying pan.

Add stock, sugar, vinegar, soy and tomato sauce, stir in and simmer vegetables for a further 3–4 minutes. Stir in cornflour and water mixture and cook until sauce becomes thick and clear.

# 16. Paprika Sauce

2 Tblsp butter
2 Tblsp flour
1½ cups milk or milk and cream
¼ tsp salt
    white pepper
2 tsp paprika
1 egg
2 Tblsp brandy

*A delicate blend of flavours to enhance shellfish.*

Melt butter in a small saucepan. Remove from heat, stir in flour, salt, pepper and paprika. Cook a minute more, remove from heat again and slowly stir in milk. Cook, stirring continuously, until sauce is smooth and thick.

Remove from heat and stir in beaten egg. Heat through again, but do not boil. Warm brandy in a separate saucepan, ignite and carefully add to sauce.

# 17. Béarnaise Sauce

3 Tblsp dry white wine or tarragon
    vinegar
1 Tblsp chopped parsley, or 1 tsp dried
    parsley
1 Tblsp chopped tarragon, or ½ tsp
    dried tarragon
1 Tblsp finely chopped shallots (optional)
1 Tblsp hot water
2 egg yolks, beaten
125 g soft butter
    lemon juice, salt and freshly-ground
    black pepper

Simmer the finely chopped herbs and shallots in wine in the top of a double boiler until reduced to 1 Tblsp.

Remove from heat and whisk in 1 Tblsp hot water and the egg yolks. Return to a low heat. Add butter, bit by bit, stirring constantly, never allowing the sauce to boil. If it does curdle, remove from heat, add 1 tsp warm water and beat vigorously.

Season with salt, pepper and lemon juice.

# 18. Sauce Parisienne

2 Tblsp butter
1½ Tblsp flour
½ cup milk
2 egg yolks
½ cup cream
  few drops lemon juice
  scant tsp salt
  white pepper
1 Tblsp Gruyère cheese, grated

Melt butter over medium heat in saucepan. Remove from heat, stir in flour then slowly add milk, stirring constantly. Add half the cream. Return to heat and simmer, stirring, until the sauce becomes thick and smooth.

Beat egg yolks with remaining cream in a small bowl. Stir in 2 Tblsp of the hot sauce, then another 2 Tblsp, and whisk this mixture back into sauce in the pan, together with the cheese. Bring to the boil and cook for a further 30 seconds. Remove from heat and season with lemon juice, salt and pepper.

# 19. Cheese Sauce

2 Tblsp butter
2 Tblsp flour
2 cups milk or milk and cream
  salt and freshly-ground black pepper
1 tsp mustard
1 cup grated Cheddar cheese

Melt butter in a small saucepan. Remove from heat and blend in flour, stirring until smooth, then add mustard and seasoning. Stir in ½ cup milk, blend in well, then add cheese and remaining milk. Return to heat and cook until thick and smooth, stirring constantly.

# 20. Mustard Sauce

2 Tblsp butter
2 heaped Tblsp flour
2 cups milk or milk and cream
2 tsp English mustard
1 Tblsp French mustard
  salt and freshly-ground black pepper
2 Tblsp capers, whole or chopped

Melt butter in a small saucepan. Remove from heat and blend in flour, stirring until smooth, then add mustard and seasoning. Stir in ½ cup milk and blend in well, then add remaining milk. Return to heat and cook, stirring constantly, until smooth and thick. Add capers and heat through.

# 21. Mustard and Orange Sauce

3 Tblsp butter
2 Tblsp chopped parsley
2 Tblsp chopped spring onions
2 tsp mustard
2 tsp grated orange rind
1 cup orange juice

*Delicious with grilled fish.*

Sauté parsley and onions in butter for 2 minutes. Add mustard, orange rind and lastly, orange juice. Simmer to reduce slightly and pour over grilled fish.

# 22. Yoghurt Herb Sauce

**4 Tblsp butter**
**1 tsp salt**
  **plenty of freshly-ground black pepper**
**1 tsp ground coriander**
**¼ tsp cardamom**
**2 Tblsp lemon juice**
**1 cup yoghurt**

*Tangy basting sauce to use with firm-fleshed grilled or barbe-cued fish.*

Melt butter in a small saucepan. Remove from heat and mix in remaining ingredients. Use to baste fish while cooking, and heat any remaining sauce to serve with the meal.

# 23. Cucumber and Cream Cheese Sauce

**250 ml cream cheese**
**2 egg yolks**
**2 Tblsp lemon juice**
**¼ tsp salt**
  **pepper**
**1 Tblsp finely chopped spring onions**
**1 cup cucumber, peeled, seeded, grated**
  **and drained of excess moisture**

*A hot sauce with an unusual blend of flavours to serve with freshly-cooked fish. Compliments from your guests are guaranteed!*

Soften cheese in a small saucepan. Blend in egg yolks, lemon juice, salt, pepper and spring onions. Cook over a low heat, stirring constantly. Add grated cucumber and heat through.

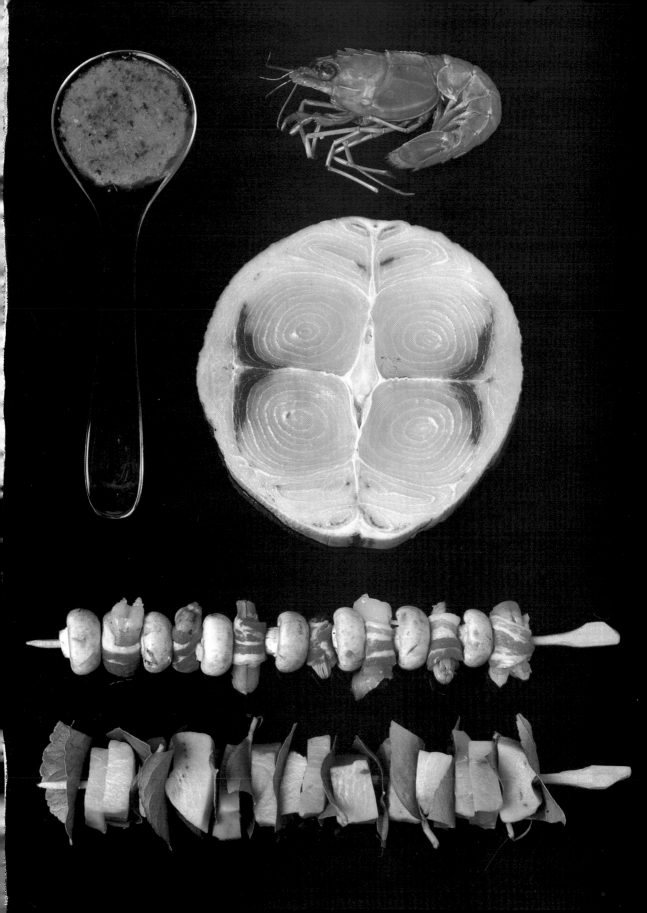

# 24. Robbeberg Stuffing

1 medium-sized onion, finely chopped
2 Tblsp butter
1 cup soft breadcrumbs
   grated rind and juice of 1 lemon
2 tsp finely-chopped savory or dried
     savory
1 egg
   salt and freshly-ground black pepper
   small tin oysters or prawns, chopped

Sauté onion in butter until soft. Add to all the other ingredients and bind with beaten egg.

# 25. Nutty Rice Stuffing

3 Tblsp olive oil
$\frac{1}{2}$ cup chopped onions
1 cup cooked rice
$\frac{1}{2}$ cup pine kernels
$\frac{1}{4}$ cup chopped hazelnuts
$\frac{1}{4}$ tsp ground cinnamon
$\frac{1}{4}$ tsp allspice
2 Tblsp sultanas
$\frac{1}{2}$ beaten egg
   salt and freshly-ground black pepper

Sauté onions in oil until soft and transparent, add rice and cook for a further few minutes. Add nuts, spices and sultanas. Mix well and blend in the egg.

# 26. Parsley Herb Stuffing

2 Tblsp butter
2 Tblsp chopped onions
1 cup chopped parsley
1 cup fresh breadcrumbs
2 Tblsp olive oil
1 egg
   pinch thyme
   salt and freshly-ground black pepper

Sauté onions in butter until soft and transparent. Stir in breadcrumbs, parsley, thyme, salt and pepper. Beat egg and olive oil together and blend into dry ingredients.

# Stuffings
# Marinades
# Basting Sauces
# and Accompaniments

# 27. Tangy Bacon and Mushroom Stuffing

125 g mushrooms ⎫
3 rashers bacon ⎬ finely chopped
1 medium onion ⎭
3 Tblsp butter
1 tsp salt
   freshly-ground black pepper
½ tsp basil
1 egg
1 cup fresh breadcrumbs

*Sufficient for one 2 kg fish, or two 750 g fish.*

Sauté mushrooms, bacon and onions in butter until tender. Add seasoning, egg and breadcrumbs and mix well.

# 28. Apple and Celery Stuffing

4 Tblsp butter
1 small chopped onion
2 chopped celery stalks
1 chopped apple
1 cup soft white breadcrumbs
1 Tblsp chopped parsley
   pinch each thyme and paprika
   salt and freshly-ground black pepper
1 egg, lightly beaten

Sauté onion and celery in butter until soft and transparent. Add apple and breadcrumbs and cook for a few minutes. Remove from heat, add parsley and seasoning and bind with the egg.

# 29. Basic Marinade and Basting Sauce

½ cup dry white wine
½ cup salad oil
1 clove garlic, crushed or chopped
½ tsp salt
½ tsp freshly-ground black pepper
1 Tblsp Worcestershire sauce
½ tsp paprika
1 Tblsp finely-chopped parsley

*For barbecuing or grilling; especially good for drier types of fish.*

# 30. Mustard Marinade

4 Tblsp oil
4 Tblsp lemon juice
1 tsp dry mustard
½ tsp curry powder
   freshly-ground black pepper
¼ tsp salt

Combine all ingredients and use as a marinade for mussels or oysters before grilling or barbecuing.

# 31. Marinade Monte-Mar

See plate 5

6 Tblsp olive oil
1 cup orange juice
2 Tblsp lemon juice
6–8 fresh orange or lemon leaves
2 cloves garlic, chopped
1 tsp oregano
2 Tblsp chopped parsley
   salt and freshly-ground black pepper

*A delicately-flavoured Portuguese marinade and basting sauce to bring the whisper of a mountain-side orange grove to your grilled or barbecued seafood.*

Combine all ingredients.

74

# 32. The Crispiest Chips

Slice or dice peeled potatoes – wash and dry well.

In a large saucepan, heat enough oil to cover chips. When hot, add chips and cook, *undisturbed* until they're crisp and golden. The secret is not to stir them at all while cooking.

Quick as a lick, remove to drain on kitchen paper and serve at once in a heated bowl. Sprinkle with salt when the chips reach the table.

# 33. Palm Bread

See plate 7

2 cups wholewheat flour
¾ cup cake flour
1½ tsp salt
1 tsp bicarbonate of soda
½ tsp garlic flakes
½ tsp oregano
1 Tblsp Parmesan cheese, grated
4 Tblsp sesame seeds
4 Tblsp sunflower seeds
2 cups (500 ml) buttermilk or yoghurt

Mix buttermilk into dry ingredients, place dough in small, round, well greased cake tin and bake at 160°C for one hour.

# 34. Garlic Bread

1 loaf French bread
  butter
3–4 cloves garlic

Cut bread into slices, and crush garlic into soft butter, mixing well. Butter bread liberally on one side, then re-form the loaf.

Wrap completely in foil and bake at 180°C for 15 minutes. Open the foil along the top of the loaf, and return to the oven for a further 5–7 minutes until the top is crisp.

# 35. Herb Bread

Follow instructions for Garlic Bread [34], replacing garlic with a sprinkling of dried mixed herbs on each slice of bread. One may, of course, use garlic and herbs together.

# 36. Green Salad (French Salad)

Toss together clean, crisp and dry lettuce – torn into pieces – finely sliced cucumber, green pepper, onion rings or sliced spring onions.

Just before serving sprinkle with French Dressing [9], and garnish with chopped parsley or chives.

COMPLIMENTARY GARNISHES: Fresh, chopped herbs such as chervil or savory, whole or chopped capers, crispy fried diced bread rubbed with garlic, diced gherkins, nasturtium leaves, hard-boiled eggs cut in quarters, sliced tomatoes, avocado pear, apple wedges, pineapple slices.

# 37. Greek Salad

Garnish a Green Salad with black olives and cubed feta cheese and add a pinch of dried, mixed herbs to the French Dressing.

# 38. Persian Rice

4 large, ripe tomatoes, peeled and sliced
175 g button mushrooms, sliced or quartered
4 spring onions
  butter
1 cup long-grained rice
4 Tblsp dry white wine
1½ cups chicken stock
  salt and freshly-ground black pepper
1 clove garlic, finely chopped
¼ tsp dried oregano
2 Tblsp finely chopped parsley

Sauté onions in 4 Tblsp butter in a medium saucepan until golden. Add garlic, tomatoes, mushrooms, salt, pepper oregano and parsley. After a minute or two stir in rice.

Pour in wine and stock. Simmer gently until all the liquid has been absorbed and the rice is cooked.

# 39. Chipattis

**1 cup semolina**
**1 cup flour**
**⅔ cup water**
**salt**

*Crispy accompaniments to any curry – and especially The Sultan's Crayfish* [111] *or curried Prawns* [105].

Mix water into dry ingredients, adding very slowly until you have a firm ball of dough. Break off pieces about the size of 1 Tblsp and roll out very thinly. Fry in 2 cm hot oil in a large frying pan until crisp and golden. Drain on absorbent paper and salt lightly on both sides. Makes 12–15.

Chipattis can be made in advance – even on the previous day – and then warmed up.

# Seafood Recipes

# 40. Alikreukels in Garlic Butter

Prepare alikreukels for cooking (see p. 22). Slice thinly or chop finely.

Heat butter until hot and foamy. Add 2–3 cloves chopped garlic, a squeeze of lemon juice, salt and freshly-ground black pepper.

Sauté Alikreukels gently in the garlic butter sauce for 2–3 minutes, being careful not to let the butter burn.

Serve on rice, with Palm Bread [33].

# 41. Barbecued Alikreukels

Place alikreukels, lying on their backs, in moderate coals to cook in their own juices. Allow 20–30 minutes, depending on size. Remove from their shells, cut off stomach and protective shell, slice and serve with Garlic Butter Sauce, [8] or French Dressing [9] as an hors d'oeuvre to your barbecue.

Perlemoen may also be barbecued in this way.

# 42. Arniston Alikreukels

*To our delight, we've found a way of using up our less-successful home-brewed beer !*

Cook alikreukels in boiling salted water, in their shells, for 15–20 minutes. Remove fish from shells, cut off stomachs and protective shells and slice finely.

Sauté a sliced onion and a chopped clove of garlic in butter, until the onion is soft and transparent. Add alikreukel slices, season with salt, freshly-ground black pepper and ½ tsp paprika. Sauté a minute more then add enough beer to cover. Simmer covered for a further five minutes and serve on a bed of rice.

# 43. Angel Fish Niçoise

6 Angel Fish steaks, about 2–3 cm thick
    flour, seasoned with salt and pepper
½ cup olive oil
4 medium-sized ripe tomatoes, skinned,
    seeded and chopped
½ cup dry white wine
12 black olives, halved and stoned
1 Tblsp anchovy paste
2 cloves garlic, crushed
2 Tblsp capers
1 Tblsp chopped tarragon or ½ tsp dried
    tarragon
3 lemons
1 can rolled anchovy fillets
    salt and freshly-ground black pepper

Coat celestial steaks lightly with seasoned flour, fry until golden brown for 2–3 minutes on each side in half the olive oil.

Cook tomatoes in remaining oil until soft. Add olives, anchovy paste, garlic, capers, tarragon and wine. Season with salt and pepper and simmer for about 5 minutes, until sauce has thickened.

Place fish steaks on hot serving platter, surround with Niçoise Sauce, decorate with rolled anchovy fillets and serve with lemon wedges.

This heavenly dish serves six small-appetited souls.

ALTERNATIVES

Cape Salmon, Kabeljou, Snoek, Tuna, Barracuda, Scotsman, Seventy Four, Yellowtail, John Brown.

# 44. Bouillabaise

See plate 6

BOUILLON

300 g onions, thinly sliced
150 g leeks, thinly sliced
½ cup olive oil
1½ litres water
½ litre dry white wine
1 kg fish bones and trimmings
1¼ kg ripe tomatoes, peeled and chopped
½ cup fresh fennel or ⅔ tsp dried fennel
2 cloves garlic, finely chopped
3 strips orange peel
½ tsp thyme
4 sprigs parsley
2 bay leaves
½ tsp saffron or turmeric
3 tsp salt
    freshly-ground black pepper

*A speciality of Marseilles, in France, its origin goes back to the mists of time. It is said that the ancient Phoenicians were the first to introduce this classical combination of fish, shellfish, white wine and herbs.*

*Bouillabaise is traditionally served with broth and fish separate, and shellfish still in their shells. It is accompanied by crusty bread.*

In a large, heavy-based saucepan sauté onions and leeks in oil until soft and transparent. Add remaining ingredients and simmer, uncovered, for 30 minutes. Check seasoning.

ROUILLE

2 green peppers, seeded and chopped
1 dry chilli pepper or a few drops tabasco
1¾ cups water
2 canned pimentos, drained
4 cloves garlic, chopped
5 Tblsp olive oil
1–3 Tblsp fine breadcrumbs

Simmer green peppers and chilli pepper in water for about 10 minutes until tender. Drain and pat dry.

Blend in a liquidiser the peppers, chilli pepper, pimentos, garlic and olive oil. Pour into a bowl and mix in sufficient breadcrumbs to make the rouille thick enough to hold its shape in a spoon. Add tabasco at this stage, if you haven't used the chilli pepper. Set aside.

SEAFOOD

2 kg firm fish, cut in cubes (Cape
    Salmon, Kabeljou, Kingklip,
    Gurnard, Monk-fish, Yellowtail,
    Stumpnose, Musselcracker, Rock
    Cod, Silver Fish – or a combination
    thereof)
500 g Prawns, slit down back and remove
    'vein'
500 g prepared Mussels, in their shells,
    beards removed
1 kg Rock Lobster, diced in large pieces
500 g eel, cut in small slices ⎫
500 g Scallops          ⎬ if available
a few Langoustine      ⎭

Strain bouillon and bring to the boil. Add fish and eel and
simmer for 5 minutes. Add rock lobster, langoustine,
prawns, scallops and mussels and simmer for a further 5
minutes, until all the seafood is cooked. Check seasoning.

If you wish to serve soup and fish together, arrange seafood in an ample tureen and ladle over the ambrosial
liquid.

Serve rouille separately.

Serves 8–10.

# 45. Mushroom and Almond Bream

See plate 8

750 g fillets of Bream
150 g butter
    flour, salt and freshly-ground black
    pepper
60 g flaked almonds
125 g button mushrooms
    squeeze of lemon juice
3 Tblsp chopped parsley
8 Tblsp thick cream

*Note: This is a super recipe for almost any fish. Smaller fish,
cooked whole, can be used, if you have the patience while
eating, to pluck out the bones.*

Season fish with salt and pepper, dip in flour and gently
shake off excess. Fry in half the butter and set aside on a
warmed serving platter.

Add remaining butter to frying pan, sauté almonds until
golden, then add mushrooms, lemon juice, 2 Tblsp parsley,
½ tsp salt and freshly-ground black pepper. Cook gently
over a low heat until mushrooms are tender. Stir in cream,
heat through and spoon sauce around fried fish. Sprinkle
with remaining parsley and serve with fluffy mashed potatoes.

Serves six.

## ALTERNATIVES

Angel Fish, Baardman, Barbel, Blacktail, Blue Hottentot,
Butter Fish, Cape Salmon, Dageraad, Elf, Frans Madame,
Grunter, Gurnard, Haarder, Jacobever, John Brown, John
Dory, Kabeljou, Kingklip, Leervis, Monkfish, Mussel-
cracker, Rock Cod, Sole, Stockfish, Scotsman, Seventy
Four, Silver Fish, White Steenbras, Zebra.

# 46. Paprika Salmon

1 kg Cape Salmon; cut into 3 cm slices
4 Tblsp melted butter
2 Tblsp chopped parsley
   squeeze of lemon juice
1 tsp salt
2 tsp paprika
¼ tsp basil
   freshly-ground black pepper
6 Tblsp cream

Mix together butter, parsley, lemon juice and seasoning.

Wash fish slices, pat dry and arrange on a pre-heated, buttered grilling pan. Spread half the sauce over the fish and grill for 3–4 minutes. Turn fish slices over, spread with remaining sauce and cook for a further 2–4 minutes until fish is cooked.

Remove fish to a heated serving platter.

Pour cream onto grilling pan on top of the stove. Mix well with buttery fish juices and pour over fish.

Serve with new boiled potatoes, tossed in butter, and a French salad [36].

Serves four to six.

ALTERNATIVES:

Yellowtail, Kabeljou, Kingklip, Angel Fish, Stockfish.

# 47. Geelbek Toutjies

*This is a traditional Cape delicacy, a toothsome fish biltong which can be eaten raw or baked.*

Clean, head and de-bone a cape salmon and cut flesh lengthways into strips 4 cm wide, leaving tail attached. Salt heavily with coarse salt and hang up to dry out in a warm place. (Cape Coloured folk make a special frame on which to attach the strips of flesh.)

After 4–6 hours wash the salt off carefully, re-salt lightly and hang up again. After a week or so your Geelbek Toutjies are ready to be eaten.

# 48. Breton Fish Soup

**1,5 kg firm fish, skinned and cut in pieces.**
  **(Cape Salmon, Kabeljou, Yellowtail,**
**Silver Fish, Musselcracker or Rock Cod)**
**⅓ cup olive oil**
**3 onions, chopped**
**4 medium-sized potatoes, sliced**
**4 ripe tomatoes, skinned and chopped**
**2 cloves garlic, finely chopped**
**1 tsp salt**
  **freshly-ground black pepper**
**1 tsp turmeric**
**Small pinch thyme**
**1 bay leaf**
**1 cup dry white wine**
**1 litre water**

*The Province of Bretagne in France takes its food and cooking simply as you'll notice if you compare this soup with the more complicated and highly seasoned Bouillabaise from Provence.*

Sauté onions and potatoes in oil until golden. Add tomatoes, garlic, fish and seasoning and simmer for 5 minutes. Pour over wine and water, bring to the boil and simmer for a further 10–15 minutes until fish and potatoes are cooked.

Serve with crisp, hot Garlic or Herb Bread [34 and 35]. Serves 8–10.

# 49. Golden Crab Pie

**25 cm Pie Plate lined with Quiche**
  **Pastry [3], baked blind.**
**1 cup white sauce**
**⅔ cup grated cheese**
**2 cups flaked crab meat, fresh or**
  **tinned**
**1 small onion, finely chopped**
**1 cup milk**
**2 eggs**
**¼ tsp salt**
  **freshly-ground black pepper to taste**
**½ tsp grated lemon rind**
**1 tsp mustard powder**
**1 scant pinch mace**
**2 Tblsp flaked almonds**

*This dish can also be made without the pastry.*

Beat eggs with milk and combine with white sauce, cheese, crab meat, onion, mustard, lemon rind and spices. Sprinkle with almonds. Add to pie crust and bake at 150°C for 30–40 minutes. Sinfully delicious!

Serves six.

84

# 50. Crab Paprika

2 cups freshly-cooked Crab meat
Paprika Sauce, [16]
toasted breadcrumbs

*A delicious entrée or late-night tiffin for four.*

Stir Crab meat into sauce, spoon into buttered scallop shells or an ovenproof dish and sprinkle generously with toasted crumbs. Bake in a hot oven until heated through and topping is crunchy.

ALTERNATIVES
Diced, cooked Lobster, Prawns or Monkfish.

# 51. Madeira Eel

*A speciality of the lush island of Madeira.*

Clean and fillet your Eel, following instructions on p. 28. Cut fish in slices, about 5 cm wide and season with salt and pepper. Peel and cut bananas into chunks to correspond with the width of fish slices. Wrap fish around bananas and secure with toothpicks. Dip in egg and breadcrumbs and deep-fry until golden brown.

ALTERNATIVES
Fillets of Sole, Kingklip, Monkfish.

# 52. Nutty-stuffed Eel

1 kg Eel, cleaned and prepared for stuffing and baking
salt and freshly-ground black pepper
Nutty Rice Stuffing, [25]
3 Tblsp butter
½ cup cream
¼ cup dry white wine

Season eel with salt and pepper, inside and out. Stuff and sew it up.

Melt butter in a baking dish, add fish and coat with melted butter. Bake at 150°C for one hour, basting occasionally and dredging the surface with a little flour.

When eel is cooked, transfer to a heated serving platter, strain baking liquor into a small saucepan, stir in cream and wine, adjust seasoning and serve sauce separately.

Serve with chips and a French Salad [36].

Serves six.

# 53. Beach party Galjoen

Dig – with your hands or a shovel – a hole in the sands of your choice, 60 cm wide and 30 cm deep. Build a blazing fire therein.

Until the hole is chockful of glowing embers, quaff a few vesselsful of your favourite tipple, then wrap your whole cleaned and seasoned galjoen in several layers of brown paper.

Place fearlessly in the middle of the embers. Cover lightly with a couple of shovelsful of sand and after about 30 minutes behold! Out you'll pull an unpretty, charred mass.

Cool it slightly, slit it open and peel off the blackened remains of its brown paper shroud, skin and scales. You'll have a fingerlicking dish fit for a king.

# 54. Gracious Gurnard

**4 Gurnard fillets**
**3 Tblsp butter**
**100 g mushrooms, sliced**
   **squeeze of lemon juice**
**2 Tblsp chopped parsley**
**1 Tblsp flour**
**2 Tblsp dry sherry**
**1 Tblsp grated Parmesan cheese**
**1 tsp tomato paste**
**¼ cup dry white wine**
**½ cup cream**
**½ cup milk**
**½ tsp salt**
   **freshly-ground black pepper**

In a medium saucepan, sauté mushrooms and parsley until mushrooms are tender. Add a squeeze of lemon juice. Stir in flour, then blend in sherry, wine, cheese and tomato paste. Slowly stir in cream, milk and seasoning and cook, stirring, for a minute or two.

Loosely roll up fish fillets, seasoned with a little salt and pepper. Place fish in sauce, spooning a little over each fillet. Simmer very gently for 6–7 minutes until fish is cooked.

Serve over rice or fluffy mashed potatoes.

Serves four.

ALTERNATIVES
Sole, Kingklip, Monkfish, Stockfish, Barbel, Shark, Skate.

# 55. South American Soused Haarders

4 small Haarders, totalling about 1 kg,
    cleaned and beheaded
6 Tblsp olive oil
2 medium-sized onions, finely sliced
2 cloves garlic, chopped
2 cups sliced black mushrooms
1 green pepper, finely sliced
2 tsp ground ginger or 3 cm piece fresh
    ginger
1 tsp salt
  freshly-ground black pepper
1 cup white vinegar
1 cup water
1 Tblsp brown sugar

Brown fish on both sides in half the oil. Season well with salt and pepper, remove from pan and set aside.

Add remaining oil and sauté onions until soft and transparent. Add garlic, mushrooms, green pepper and ginger, sauté for 2 minutes more, then pour in water, vinegar and sugar. Simmer slowly for 2–3 minutes.

Return fish to marinade, simmer for five minutes, remove from the heat, cool and chill overnight before serving.

Serves four.

ALTERNATIVES:

Maasbanker, Mackerel, Pilchard

# 56. Smoky Mountain Pancake Rolls    See plate 8

**PANCAKES**

3 eggs
1 cup milk
¾ cup flour
¼ tsp salt

**FILLING**

Mix together . . .
2 medium-sized smoked Haarders,
    skinned, de-boned and flaked
    (or substitute a similar quantity of
    any other smoked fish)
250 g smooth cottage cheese
1 apple, grated
1 small onion, grated
  freshly ground black pepper
  pinch cayenne pepper
4 Tblsp chopped parsley

*A deliciously different cold hors d'oeuvre or luncheon dish.*
    *Instead of smoked fish, one may substitute one 200 g can of salmon or tuna.*

Sift flour and salt into bowl, break in eggs and half the milk, mix until smooth, then add remaining milk.

Make wafer thin pancakes and allow them to cool. Stack with a sprinkling of cold water between each.

Spread filling over each pancake, roll up and decorate with lemon twists and sprigs of parsley.

Serves eight as hors d'oeuvres or four as a luncheon dish.

# 57. Rollmops

See plate 4

24 Herring fillets
450 ml cider vinegar
450 ml cold water
3 Tblsp hot prepared mustard
2 Tblsp capers
3 small onions, thinly sliced into rings
3 dill pickled cucumbers
12 whole black peppercorns, bruised
6 whole allspice
6 whole cloves
3 small bay leaves

Sterilise glass (not metal) pickling jar with boiling water. Rinse herring fillets under cold running water, drain on thick absorbent paper then pat dry. Discard any remaining bones if you have the patience – and a pair of tweezers!

Put vinegar, water, allspice, cloves, peppercorns and bay leaves into a saucepan. Bring to the boil and simmer uncovered for five minutes. Cool to room temperature.

Lay herring fillets skin side down and spread each one sparingly with mustard. Cut dill pickled cucumber into wedges lengthwise. At the narrow end of each fillet place a few onion rings, 3–4 capers and a wedge of dill pickle. Roll fillets up and secure with toothpicks. Pack them in layers in container, scattering a few onion rings between the layers and on top.

Pour marinade over, seal or cover with plastic and refrigerate for 5–7 days before serving.

Serve as an hors d'oeuvre, garnished with onion rings and parsley.

# 58. John Dory Meunière

Clean one John Dory per person, leaving head and tail in situ. Season with salt and pepper, dip in flour and fry in foamy hot butter until cooked through.

Remove to heated serving platter, add more butter to the pan, together with a few tablespoonfuls chopped parsley. Pour parsley butter over fish, sprinkle with toasted, flaked almonds and serve at once garnished with lemon wedges.

Serve with new potatoes tossed in parsley butter.

ALTERNATIVES:

Any suitable sized Sole, Blacktail, Blue Hottentot, Bream, Butter Fish, Dageraad, Elf, Frans Madame, Grunter, Haarder, Streepie, Scotsman, Seventy Four, Zebra, John Brown, Jacobever, Silver Fish.

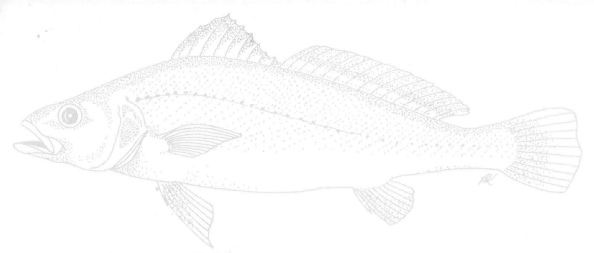

# 59. Kabeljou Mornay

750 g cooked Kabeljou, filleted and
   cut into slices
Mornay Sauce, [10]
Parmesan Cheese, grated

*Note:* Cheese Sauce [19],
  makes a good substitute for
  Mornay Sauce.

*A deliciously simple way to dress up freshly-cooked fish or any left-over fish.*

Lay fish in a buttered casserole dish, pour over sauce, coating fish well. Sprinkle generously with Parmesan cheese and bake at 180°C for about 20 minutes until fish is heated through and topping is crisp and golden.
    Serve with a Green Salad and crisp Garlic or Herb Bread, [36, 34 and 35].
    Serves six.

## ALTERNATIVES

Kingklip, Monkfish, Rock Cod, Silverfish, Barbel, Cape Salmon, Gurnard, Hottentot, Musselcracker, Rock Lobster, Shark, Stockfish.

# 60. Cheat's Fish Thermidor

750 g Kabeljou
½ cup milk
   salt and freshly-ground black pepper
400 g tin mushroom soup
2 Tblsp dry sherry
2 Tblsp brandy (optional)
½ cup finely grated Cheddar cheese

Skin fish, remove bones and cut into serving portions. Season with salt and pepper, place in baking dish and pour over milk. Bake, uncovered for 20 minutes at 175°C. Strain off liquid.
    Combine undiluted soup, sherry, brandy and baking liquid in small saucepan. Bring to the boil stirring constantly, then pour over baked fish. Sprinkle cheese on top and return to the oven for 5–6 minutes to brown under the grill.
    Serve with baked potatoes and a Green Salad [36].
    Serves six.

## ALTERNATIVES

Angel Fish, Bream, Gurnard, Hottentot, John Dory, Kingklip, Stockfish.

# 61. Wine-baked Kingklip with Asparagus

500 g Kingklip fillets
⅓ cup dry white wine
460 g can asparagus spears
  salt and freshly-ground black pepper
2 Tblsp butter
1 small onion finely chopped
2 Tblsp flour
3 Tblsp cream
  chopped parsley
  Fluffy mashed potatoes

Drain asparagus, reserving liquid. Arrange with fish fillets in a buttered, ovenproof dish. Season well with salt and pepper, pour over wine, cover tightly with foil and bake at 180°C until fish is cooked – about 15–20 minutes.

Melt butter in small saucepan. Sauté onion until transparent. Remove from heat, stir in flour and asparagus liquid. Season with salt and pepper. Cook, stirring, until the sauce boils and thickens. Add cream and liquid from baked fish. Heat through.

Arrange fish and asparagus spears on a serving platter.

Surround with fluffy mashed potatoes, pour sauce over fish and garnish with chopped parsley.

Serves four.

ALTERNATIVES:

Angel Fish, Cape Salmon, Gurnard, Kabeljou, Monkfish, Musselcracker, Rock Cod, Stockfish, Shark, Red Steenbras,

# 62. Shantung Kingklip

500 g Kingklip fillets
  salt and white pepper
  flour
  Shantung Batter, [5]

Season fish well with salt and pepper. Dip in flour and shantung batter and fry in hot oil until crispy brown.

Serves four.

ALTERNATIVES:

Kabeljou, Rock Cod.

# 63. Jugged Kippers

*This is the simplest method of preparing smoked kippers, and you'll have no pans to clean !*

Place kippers, heads-down, in a deep jug. Fill with boiling water, leave for five minutes, then drain well and serve, with a knob of butter.

# 64. Smoked Kipper Pâté

See plate 7

250 g smoked, boneless kippers
100 g butter
1 clove garlic, finely chopped
2 tsp anchovy paste (optional)
freshly-ground black pepper
4 Tblsp cream

*This delicious, quick-to-make pâté can also be used as a sandwich filling, to top savouries or to stuff eggs or tomatoes. It keeps well for up to a week in the fridge.*

Place kippers heads-down, in a deep jug. Fill with boiling water, leave for 5 minutes then drain, cool and flake flesh.

Melt butter in a small saucepan. Gently fry garlic for a minute or two. Add flaked fish, anchovy paste, pepper and cream and mix well. Blend in a liquidiser.

# 65. Mustard-marinated Langoustine

16 Langoustine, washed and dried, in their shells
Mustard Marinade, [30] (double quantity)
125 ml cream

Cut each langoustine in half. Remove the 'worm'.

Place, shell down, on pre-heated grilling tray. Brush each half with mustard marinade and grill for 5–6 minutes until just cooked through.

Place in warmed serving dish.

Pour any remaining marinade into grilling tray, heat on the top of the stove, pour in cream and heat through, stirring.

Pour over langoustine and serve with Persian Rice [38].

Serves four.

*Note:* Rock lobster and prawns are equally delicious with this mustard marinade treatment.

# 66. Mustard Maasbanker

4 Maasbankers, cleaned, beheaded and ready for baking
2 Tblsp butter
½ Tblsp English mustard
1 Tblsp French mustard
1 Tblsp tomato puree
¼ tsp brown sugar
4 Tblsp cream
¼ tsp mixed herbs
½ tsp salt
freshly-ground black pepper

Place 1 Tblsp butter in an ovenproof dish and pop in oven for a few moments to melt.

Mix mustard, tomato purée, sugar, cream and seasoning. Place fish side by side in the buttered dish, pour over mustard sauce and bake at 180°C for 15–20 minutes, turning fish once during the cooking process.

Garnish with lemon wedges and a little chopped parsley and serve with boiled new potatoes tossed in butter.

Serves four.

ALTERNATIVES

Mackerel, Spanish Mackerel, Haarder, Herring.

# 67. Soused Mackerel

See plate 4

4 whole Mackerel, totalling about 1 kg, cleaned and beheaded (or 2 larger fish
2 medium-sized onions, finely sliced
2 Tblsp chopped parsley
2 bay leaves
2 cloves
  pinch thyme
12 whole black peppercorns
2 tsp salt
2 cups white vinegar
1 cup water
2 Tblsp lemon juice
  parsley sprigs for decorating

Lay fish side by side in a shallow baking dish. Season with salt and thyme, scatter over them onions, parsley, bay leaves, cloves and peppercorns.

Mix vinegar, water and lemon juice and pour over fish. Bake covered at 160°C for about 25 minutes until fish are firm to touch. Allow longer for larger fish. Cool, then chill and marinate overnight, covered.

To serve, remove fish from sousing liquid and garnish with sprigs of parsley.

Serves four.

ALTERNATIVES

Haarder, Maasbanker, Pilchard.

# 68. Mackerel with Mustard and Orange Sauce

4 small whole Mackerel, cleaned, washed and split down backbone
3 Tblsp oil
½ tsp paprika
  salt and freshly-ground black pepper
2 oranges, sliced
  Mustard and Orange Sauce, [21]

Place fish on a pre-heated grilling pan and brush with oil. Season with salt, pepper and paprika and grill for 15–20 minutes until golden brown, turning once during cooking.

Arrange on heated serving platter while brewing the sauce.

Pour sauce over hot fish, garnish with orange slices and serve at once.

Serves four.

ALTERNATIVES:

Maasbanker, Elf, Haarder.

# 69. Swordfish Kebabs Monte-Mar

See plate 5

1 kg Marlin or Swordfish, cut in 4 cm cubes
Marinade Monte-Mar, [31]
fresh orange or lemon leaves

Season fish with salt and freshly-ground black pepper and marinate for 2 hours at room temperature. Thread fish cubes onto skewers, with fresh leaves in between.

Grill or barbecue over medium coals, for 5–6 minutes on each side, basting with the marinade. Remove to a heated serving platter, strain marinade, heat and serve separately.

Serve kebabs on a bed of rice with a Green Salad [36] garnished with black olives.

Serves six.

ALTERNATIVES:

Tuna, Angel Fish.

92

# 70. Moules Marinière

4–6 dozen freshly-gathered Mussels
1 medium-sized onion, chopped
1 small clove garlic, chopped
1 Tblsp butter
3 Tblsp chopped parsley
1 cup dry white wine
½ cup water
    bouquet garni made of 4 parsley sprigs,
      1 sprig of thyme and 1 bay leaf
      (or substitute one commercial dried
      bouquet garni)
    freshly-ground black pepper
3 Tblsp cream

*A favourite dish in France; a delicious flavour combination of Mussels, white wine and herbs served with crusty Garlic Bread [34] and icy cold dry white wine.*

Soak mussels in fresh water for half an hour, then scrub shells clean and pull out beards.

Sauté onion and garlic in butter until soft and transparent then stir in parsley, wine, water, bouquet garni, salt and pepper. Simmer uncovered for 10 minutes. Add mussels, cover and steam until they open. Discard any which remain shut. Remove one shell from each mussel and discard. Arrange mussels in a large, deep serving platter and keep warm.

Strain sauce into a small saucepan, boil quickly to reduce by half, stir in cream then remove from heat. Correct seasoning and pour over the mussels.

Garnish with generously scattered chopped parsley and serve at once.

Serves 6–8.

# 71. Perfect Mussel Soup

See plate 8

36 steamed, prepared Mussels (see p. 38)
    cut in half (Reserve liquor)
1 medium onion, sliced
2–3 Tblsp chopped parsley
1 small clove garlic, chopped
3 Tblsp butter
3½ Tblsp flour
2½ cups milk
½ cup mussel liquor
½ cup water
½ cup dry white wine
½ chicken stock cube, crumbled
    freshly-ground black pepper
    pinch oregano
1 bay leaf

*In this recipe it is essential to keep exactly to the amount of seasoning specified and the quantities of water, mussel liquor and wine. It's so easy to ruin the delicate flavour of mussels.*

Sauté onion, garlic and parsley in butter until soft. Stir in flour and stock cube. Slowly add milk, water, liquor and wine and return to heat, stirring constantly until soup is smooth and thickened. Add seasoning. Simmer with the lid on for 10 minutes.

Add mussels, heat through, and serve with Palm Bread, [33].

Serves six.

# 72. Pickled Mussels

See plate 4

Clean and steam open mussels as described on p. 38. Reserve strained mussel liquor from the steaming process.

Use two quantities of liquor to one quantity of white vinegar and add one bay leaf and one chopped, dried chilli.

Place mussels in a sterilised, airtight glass container and cover with the pickling liquid. Add 5 mm olive oil which will float on the surface and keep the mussels air-tight. Screw on lid and keep refrigerated.

Pickled mussels improve with age and will keep for up to six weeks. They make delicious snacks on biscuits or just as they are.

# 73. Barbecued Mussels

*Two unusual hors d'oeuvre to enjoy before your fish braai.*

Place freshly-gathered, scrubbed mussels round the edges of your braai grid.

Remove from heat as soon as they open and serve, piping hot, dipped in:

French dressing [9] or
Hot Garlic Butter [8].

# 74. Marinated Mussels

**About 24 mussels**
**Mustard Marinade, [30]**

Clean and steam open mussels. (See p. 38). Remove one shell and the beard, leaving mussels attached to the other shell. Make sure they're free of sand.

Spoon a little marinade into each mussel shell. Marinate for 30 minutes, then place carefully round the edges of the barbecue grid or grill in the oven until the marinade bubbles and the mussel is heated through.

Serves 4–6.

ALTERNATIVE:

Oysters.

# 75. Snow Goose Mussels

250 g Mussels (about 35), cleaned,
    steamed open and removed from
    their shells
2 Tblsp butter
4 Tblsp finely-chopped parsley
2 scant Tblsp flour
1 cup milk
⅓ cup dry white wine
½ chicken stock cube
    freshly-ground black pepper
    Fluffy mashed potatoes

Sauté parsley in butter for a minute or two. Remove from heat, stir in flour, then add milk. Return to heat and cook, stirring, until sauce thickens. Add wine, crumbled stock cube and ground black pepper to taste. Add mussels and heat through.

Pipe mashed potatoes around the edges of four scallop shells. Carefully spoon Snow Goose Mussels into the centres and sprinkle with chopped parsley.

If you wish to make these hors d'oeuvres beforehand, heat in a hot oven for about 10 minutes, then garnish with parsley.

Serves four.

# 76. Pandora's Mussels

36 Mussels, steamed open, cleaned and
    cut into thirds (Reserve liquor)
1 cup finely chopped onion
½ cup butter
3 cups soft breadcrumbs
¼ tsp freshly-ground black pepper
⅛ tsp thyme
¼ tsp marjoram
¼ tsp salt
¼ cup liquid from cooked mussels
½ cup pine kernels
    squeeze of lemon juice

Sauté onion in butter unt l soft and transparent, add chopped mussels, breadcrumbs, salt, pepper, herbs, pine kernels, lemon juice and mussel liquid.

Pack six scallop shells with mussel mixture, sprinkle with topping and bake at 180°C for 10–15 minutes until heated through and topping is crispy brown.

Garnish with sprigs of parsley and a twist of lemon.

Serves six.

## TOPPING

½ cup melted butter ⎤
1 cup soft breadcrumbs ⎬ combined
¼ cup chopped parsley ⎦

# 77. Red Sails in the Sunset

1 kg fresh, scrubbed Mussels
¼ kg Prawns, shelled
½ cup dry white wine
1 cup water
1 cup chopped shallots or spring onions
¼ cup chopped celery
2 cups ripe tomatoes, peeled and
    chopped (or substitute canned
    tomatoes)
½ chicken stock cube
2 bay leaves
  freshly-ground black pepper
1 Tblsp chopped parsley

In a large saucepan place wine, water, shallots, celery, tomatoes, bay leaves, pepper and stock cube. Simmer slowly for 10 minutes to develop the flavour.

Add mussels, prawns and cover tightly, and simmer gently for a few minutes more until mussels open and prawns are cooked. Remove mussel beards.

Sprinkle with chopped parsley and serve with hot Garlic Bread [34].

Serves four.

# 78. Intoxicated Octopus

1 large Octopus or 2 small ones,
    totalling about 1 kg
½ cup olive oil
1½ cups chopped onions
2 large cloves garlic, crushed
4 Tblsp tomato puree
1 cup dry red wine
½ cup water
1 chicken stock cube
2 bay leaves
½ tsp oregano
  freshly-ground black pepper
½ tsp salt
18 new potatoes, peeled

Following instructions on p. 40 clean, skin, tenderise and cook octopus. Cut into bite-sized chunks.

Sauté onions in olive oil until golden. Add octopus, garlic, tomato purée, wine, water, crumbled stock cube, bay leaves, oregano, salt and plenty of pepper. Simmer very slowly for 10 minutes. Add potatoes and simmer a further 15–20 minutes until cooked through and octopus is tender.

Serve with hot Garlic Bread [34] and a Greek Salad [37].

Serves six.

# 79. Pickled Octopus

500 g Octopus, cleaned and cooked.
See p. 40. (We usually use the very
ends of the tentacles for pickling.)
1 cup cider vinegar
1 cup water
½ cup chopped spring onions
12 peppercorns
6 whole allspice
6 cloves
3 small bay leaves

Cut octopus into small pieces. Mix remaining ingredients together, add octopus and fill sterilised airtight pickling jars or screwtop glass bottles, adding more vinegar and water in equal quantities if necessary. Seal tops with a film of olive oil, close and store for at least one week before serving.

Keep refrigerated indefinitely and use for pre-dinner snacks.

# 80. Oysters Mornay

Place clean, opened oysters on a layer of coarse salt on a baking tray. Sprinkle over a topping of mild grated cheese mixed with fine breadcrumbs. Grill for 2–3 minutes until topping is crisp and serve at once.

# 81. Deep-fried Oysters

Remove oysters from their shells; dip in milk then seasoned flour, deep fry in hot oil, drain on absorbent paper. Garnish with sprigs of parsley and lemon wedges.

# 82. Oysters Kilpatrick

24 Oysters
4 bacon rashers
Worcestershire Sauce

Place clean, opened oysters on a layer of coarse salt on a baking tray. Chop bacon finely and place a teaspoonful atop each oyster.

Sprinkle a few drops of Worcestershire sauce on each and grill until bacon is crisp. Serve hot.

Serves four as an hors d'oeuvre.

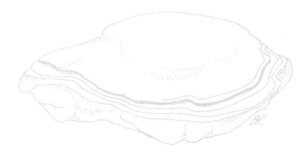

# 83. Devilled Oysters on Skewers

Remove oysters from shells, thread onto skewers, dip in melted butter seasoned with a squeeze of lemon juice, salt and pepper. Roll in fine breadcrumbs seasoned with a pinch of cayenne pepper and grill or barbecue for 3–4 minutes.

Serve with lemon wedges.

# 84. Nutty-crusted Oysters

¼ cup flour
¼ tsp ground black pepper
½ tsp allspice
16–20 Oysters, cleaned and drained
2 eggs, beaten
⅔ cup dry breadcrumbs
⅓ cup finely chopped walnuts
  oil for deep frying

*Deep-fried oysters with a most mouth-watering crusting !*

Combine flour, pepper and allspice. Dip oysters into this mixture and set aside for 15 minutes.

Combine crumbs and walnuts, then dip flour-coated oysters in beaten egg and then in crumbs and walnut mixture. Deep fry in hot oil for one minute. Drain and serve at once.

# 85. Periwinkle Capers

Following instructions on p. 41, prepare periwinkles until you have 1½ cups of cleaned shellfish.

Make Mornay Sauce [10], (omitting sherry) and add 2 Tblsp chopped capers.

Mix periwinkles into sauce, spoon into individual scallop shells sprinkle with toasted breadcrumbs and brown crisply under the grill.

Serve with lemon wedges and Palm Bread [33].

Serves four.

# 86. Pickled Winkles

See plate 4

750 g Periwinkles, cleaned and prepared.
  See p. 41.
1½ cups cider vinegar
1½ cups cold water
24 peppercorns
12 whole allspice
10 cloves
6 small bay leaves
1 cup chopped spring onions
2 Tblsp chopped chives

Rinse prepared periwinkles under running water then place in a colander and pour boiling water over them.

Combine remaining ingredients, mix well, add periwinkles and store in sterilised airtight pickling jars or screwtop glass containers. If necessary, fill jars with equal quantities water and vinegar. Pour a little olive oil in to seal the top, close and refrigerate for at least one week before serving.

Use as snacks or as a garnish for seafood salads.


# 87. Crispy-fried Perlemoen

4 medium Perlemoen, sliced into steaks
  and tenderised.
  flour, seasoned with salt and freshly-
    ground black pepper
Batter [recipes 4–6] or toasted breadcrumbs
  Lemon wedges and parsley for
    garnishing

Dip each piece of perlemoen in flour, then in batter or crumbs. Deep fry in medium hot oil and butter for about 3–4 minutes, doing only a few pieces at a time so as not to overcrowd the pan.

When crisp and golden, drain on kitchen paper and place on warmed serving platter.

A feast for four with chips and a salad, or hors d'oeuvres for 6–8.


# 88. Perlemoen Peperonata

4 medium Perlemoen, cleaned,
  cut into steaks and tenderised
3 Tblsp butter
700 g tomatoes, skinned, seeded and
  chopped
3 medium-sized onions, finely sliced
1 large green pepper, finely sliced
3 cloves garlic, finely chopped
1½ tsp salt
  plenty of freshly-ground black pepper
1 tsp fresh, chopped basil or ½ tsp
  dried basil
½ cup dry white wine

Sauté perlemoen steaks in butter in a large saucepan until nicely browned. (This is very important to the flavour of the dish.) Add onions and brown, then mix in garlic, tomatoes, green pepper and seasoning. Cover and simmer as slowly as possible for about one hour until perlemoen is tender, adding wine if the sauce becomes too dry.

Serve on a bed of rice with Greek Salad [37] and crisp Herb or Garlic Bread [34, 35].

Serve 6–8.

# 89. Alikreukel Peperonata

Follow recipe for Perlemoen Peperonata, but cook alikreukels separately, in their shells, in boiling water for 15–20 minutes. Clean, slice and add to peperonata sauce to simmer for about $\frac{1}{2}$ hour.

# 90. Mussel Peperonata

Follow recipe for Perlemoen Peperonata, adding prepared, steamed mussels in half their shell to peperonata sauce to heat through.

# 91. Octopus Peperonata

Follow recipe for Perlemoen Peperonata, adding prepared, cooked octopus to sauce to simmer for about $\frac{1}{2}$ hour.

# 92. Squid Peperonata

Add cleaned, sliced squid to peperonata sauce and simmer for about 1 hour until tender.

# 93. Mixed Seafood Peperonata

Mix fish, shellfish and molluscs of your choice, and add to peperonata sauce.

# 94. Perlemoen Ballen

750 g Perlemoen
1 small onion, chopped
Thick white sauce, made with 2 Tblsp
    butter, 2 scant Tblsp flour, 1 cup
    milk, salt and pepper
1½ Tblsp chopped parsley
½ tsp dried tarragon
½ tsp salt
    pepper to taste
2 eggs
1 Tblsp milk
    toasted breadcrumbs
    lemon wedges for garnishing

Mince perlemoen and onion very finely, then mix together with white sauce, parsley, tarragon, salt, pepper and one egg.

Form into 50 mm balls and coat with crumbs. The easiest way to do this is to fill a small bowl half way up with toasted crumbs, drop a perlemoen ballen in and rotate the bowl. Refrigerate the ballen for about 2 hours to chill.

Beat the remaining egg with 1 Tblsp milk, dip each ballen into this then re-coat with crumbs as before. Deep fry in hot oil until crisp and cooked through. Serve with lemon wedges.

This recipe makes 20 ballen which can be made the day before, kept refrigerated and deep fried just before serving. Serves six.

ALTERNATIVES:

Minced, prepared Octopus, finely chopped Prawns or Lobster.

# 95. "Paarl Lemoen"

5–6 Perlemoen, cleaned, pounded lightly
    and cut into large dice
1 cup water
¼ cup dry white wine
3 Tblsp butter
    salt and freshly-ground black pepper
    squeeze of lemon juice
1 cup soft breadcrumbs
¼ tsp nutmeg

*An adaptation of a classic Old Cape Dutch recipe, written about 1890.*

Simmer perlemoen very slowly in water, wine, butter, lemon juice, salt and pepper for 1½–2 hours in a covered saucepan until tender.

Stir in breadcrumbs and simmer until gravy is smooth and thick. Add a little more water if necessary.

Serve as an hors d'oeuvre in perlemoen shells.
Serve 6–8.

# 96. Perlemoen Parmigiani

6 medium Perlemoen
2 eggs
½ tsp salt
¼ tsp black pepper
¾ cup toasted breadcrumbs
⅓ cup Parmesan cheese, grated
⅓ cup olive oil
2 Tblsp tomato paste
2 cups ripe tomatoes, peeled and
    chopped, or substitute canned
    tomatoes
4 Tblsp dry red wine
125 g sliced black olives
200 g mild cheese, sliced or grated

Slice perlemoen into steaks and beat with a mallet until tender. Beat eggs with seasoning and mix crumbs with Parmesan cheese. Heat oil in a large frying pan, dip perlemoen steaks into egg, then crumb mixture and fry for 1 minute on each side. Add more oil if necessary.

Arrange perlemoen in a buttered baking dish, mix tomato paste, tomatoes and wine and spoon this mixture over. Dot with sliced olives, top with cheese and brown under the grill for about 4 minutes.

Serve with a Green Salad [36] and hot crusty Herb Bread [35].

Serves 6–8.

# 97. Baked Pilchards with Spicy Tomato Sauce

6 Pilchards
2 Tblsp lemon juice
    salt and freshly-ground black pepper
Spicy Tomato Sauce, [11]
chopped parsley

Clean pilchards, cut in two lengthways and remove bones. Season with salt and pepper, sprinkle with lemon juice and bake, uncovered, for about 15 minutes until cooked.

Transfer to a heated serving dish, pour over hot Spicy Tomato Sauce, sprinkle with chopped parsley and serve at once.

A tangy hors d'oeuvre for 4–6.

# 98. Sweet and Sour Prawns

500 g Prawns, cleaned, shelled and de-
    veined. Leave the last tail segment
    shell attached.
    milk
    flour, seasoned with salt and white
    pepper
Sweet and Sour Sauce, [15]

Dip prawns in milk then in seasoned flour, holding them by their tails. Deep fry in hot oil until crisp and golden. This will only take a minute or two. Drain on kitchen paper and place on a heated serving platter.

Serve on fluffy boiled rice with hot Sweet and Sour Sauce separately.

Serves 4–6.

*Note:* Make this into a more economical dish by mixing prawns with fish, or by adding cubes of chicken or pork.

ALTERNATIVES:

Cubes of Angel Fish, Cape Salmon, Eel, Gurnard, Kabeljou, Monkfish, Rock Lobster, Yellowtail, Kingklip.

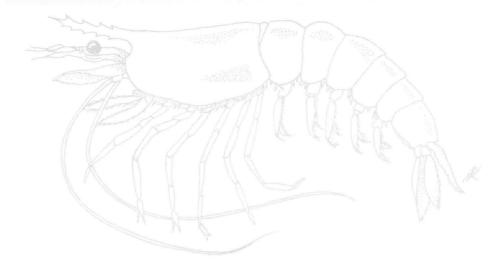

# 99. Garlic-kissed Prawns

30–36 Prawns, prepared for grilling
   (in or out of their shells)
8 Tblsp butter
8 Tblsp olive oil
2½ tsp lemon juice
¼ cup finely-chopped spring onions
2½ tsp finely-chopped garlic
   salt and freshly-ground black pepper
3 Tblsp chopped parsley
   lemon wedges for garnishing

Preheat grill. Melt butter and olive oil in a shallow baking dish just large enough to hold the prawns in one layer. Stir in lemon juice, onions, garlic, salt and pepper.

Add prawns, turning until they're well coated. Grill 12 cm from the heat for 4–5 minutes on each side, until cooked. (Prawns in shells will take a little longer.)

Transfer to a clean, heated serving dish, pour over the garlic sauce, sprinkle with chopped parsley and garnish with lemon wedges.

Serve with Persian Rice [38] Herb Bread [35] and a Green Salad [36].

Serves six.

ALTERNATIVE:

Langoustine.

# 100. Prawn Mousse Carmichael

½ cup fish or chicken stock
4 Tblsp dry white wine
500 g prawns, shelled and de-veined
1 Tblsp gelatine
4 Tblsp cold water
1 Tblsp fresh tarragon or 1 tsp dried
   tarragon
1 Tblsp tomato puree
1 Tblsp lemon juice
   salt and white pepper
1 cup cream

Oil a 1,7 litre fish mould and drain on kitchen paper.

Bring stock and wine to the boil in a small saucepan, drop the prawns in and cook for 3–4 minutes.
Remove and set aside.

Mix gelatine in 4 Tblsp cold water in a cup and stand it in a bowl of hot water until dissolved.

Liquidise prawns, stock and tarragon. Add tomato purée, lemon juice and salt and pepper to taste. Refrigerate mousse to thicken slightly.

Whip cream, fold into the mousse, pour into mould and refrigerate for at least 2 hours.

Serves four, or eight as an hors d'oeuvre.

ALTERNATIVES:

Shrimps, fresh or tinned, or tinned Salmon.

# 101. Prawns Mykonos

25–30 Prawns, shelled and de-veined
5 Tblsp olive oil
1 small onion, finely chopped
4 medium-sized tomatoes, peeled, seeded and chopped
6 Tblsp dry white wine
2 Tblsp chopped parsley
½ tsp oregano
   salt and freshly-ground black pepper
75 g feta cheese, cut into small cubes

Sauté onion in oil in a heavy frying pan until soft and transparent. Stir in tomatoes, wine, 1 Tblsp parsley and seasoning. Cook briskly uncovered until the mixture thickens to a light purée.

Add prawns and cook for 3–4 minutes, by which time they'll be firm and pink. Overcook at your peril!

Stir in cheese, sprinkle remaining parsley and serve with rice, Herb or Garlic Bread [34, 35] and a Greek Salad [37].

Serves four.

ALTERNATIVE:

Langoustine.

# 102. Prawns Peri-peri

500 g Prawns, de-headed and de-veined
¼ tsp peri-peri powder
   butter
   salt

Place prawns side by side in a baking dish just large enough to accommodate them comfortably. Add enough water to cover the bottom of the dish, sprinkle with peri-peri powder and salt and dot generously with butter.

Grill for 4–5 minutes on each side, turning once during cooking process.

Remove cooked prawns to heated serving platter, reduce peri-peri sauce quickly on top of the stove, adding a little more butter if necessary.

Serve with fluffy rice and peri-peri sauce separately.

Serves four.

# 103. Quissico Seafood Bisque

2 medium-sized onions, chopped
2 Tblsp butter
850 ml Fish Stock [2]
200 g prawns, fresh or tinned, shelled and de-veined
1 medium-sized potato
1 small tin crabmeat
¾ cup cream
1 small tin button mushrooms, or fresh mushrooms
1½ doz oysters (tinned will do, but not smoked)
   scant ½ tsp salt
   freshly-ground black pepper
2 Tblsp chopped parsley

*Extravagant, but really special!*

Sauté onion in butter until transparent. Add fish stock, prawns, salt, pepper, thinly sliced potato and crab. Bring to the boil and simmer for 5–10 minutes until the potato is tender.

Cool, then liquidise until smooth.

Return to saucepan, add cream, thinly-sliced mushrooms and oysters, whole or cut into halves, as you prefer. Heat through and garnish with chopped parsley.

Serve with Palm Bread [33].

Serves 8–10.

# 104. Shellfish and Bacon Kebabs

See plate 5

500 g Shellfish (Prawns, Langoustine,
    Rock Lobster, Scallops, Mussels)
8 rashers bacon
20 large button mushrooms, washed and
    dried
6 Tblsp butter
¼ cup lemon juice
2 cloves garlic, crushed
    salt and freshly-ground black pepper

Clean shellfish and remove from shells. Season with salt and pepper. Cut lobster and langoustine into large dice, leave prawns, scallops and mussels whole.

Cut bacon rashers into thirds, removing rind. Wrap strips round each piece of shellfish, securing with toothpicks.

Thread on to skewers, interspersed with mushrooms.

Melt butter, add crushed garlic, lemon juice and seasoning. Brush over each kebab, and grill over medium coals for 5–7 minutes until shellfish is cooked and bacon is crisp.

Serve with Persian Rice, [38].

Serves four.

# 105. Curried Prawns

500 g Prawns, peeled and de-veined
300 g butter
1 clove garlic, finely chopped
1 tsp Curry Mixture (below)
¼ cup water

### CURRY MIXTURE

1½ Tblsp chilli powder
½ Tblsp turmeric
½ Tblsp cumin
½ Tblsp coriander
½ Tblsp ground ginger
¼ tsp cardamom (optional)
¼ tsp ground cinnamon
¾ tsp ground cloves

*Blend your own spices to create a very special curry powder which may be stored for use in any curried seafood or chicken.*

Melt butter over a medium-low heat in a large frying pan. Sauté garlic for a minute or two then add curry mixture. Gently fry half the prawns at a time, so as not to over-crowd the pan. 10 cm prawns need to be cooked for 1½ minutes on each side; allow less time for smaller prawns. Transfer them to a heated platter while the rest are being done. Stir in water, simmer one minute.

Arrange on a bed of fluffy rice, spoon over the sauce and decorate with a sprig of parsley.

Serve with Chipattis [39], chopped bananas dredged in desiccated coconut and a salad of finely chopped tomatoes, green peppers and spring onions.

Serves four.

# 106. Lobster Newburg

3 medium-sized Rock Lobsters
125 g butter
120 ml brandy or cognac
1 Tblsp flour
250 ml cream
    salt and freshly-ground black pepper
    cayenne pepper
    paprika

Remove all flesh from lobster tails and bodies, and dice into 2½ cm cubes.

Warm butter in pan, add lobster and cook gently for about 3 minutes. If using cooked flesh, merely heat through. Pour over brandy, remove from heat and ignite. Gently blend in flour then add cream, salt, pepper and a pinch of cayenne pepper.

Return to heat and cook, stirring gently, for a few minutes more; just long enough to thicken slightly. Place in a warmed serving dish and sprinkle with paprika.

Serve on rice with tossed Green Salad [36].

Serves four.

# 107. Lobster Thermidor

6 cooked Rock Lobsters
Mornay Sauce, [10] made with cream or
    half cream and half milk. Increase
    dry sherry to 8 Tblsp and mustard
    to 2 level tsp
1½ Tblsp Worcestershire sauce
    pinch cayenne pepper
6 Tblsp Parmesan cheese
    fine breadcrumbs
    paprika
    butter

Cut lobsters in half lengthways. Remove flesh from tail, body and legs, dice in large cubes and reserve the shells.

Heat Mornay Sauce and blend in Worcestershire sauce and a pinch of cayenne pepper. Simmer for 2 minutes, add diced lobster flesh and heat through.

Fill shells with lobster mixture, sprinkle generously with Parmesan cheese mixed with fine breadcrumbs, dust with paprika, dot with butter and grill for a few minutes to crisp the topping.

Serve with a Green Salad [36].

Serves six.

# 108. Grilled Crayfish

Place whole, fresh crayfish on tummy, tail outstretched. Rest a large, sharp knife down the length of the back, from the horn. Hit with a mallet to split shell. Then cut tail by holding back firmly, and pushing knife hard. Leave the last tail segment joined.

Open crayfish, scrape out entrails with a teaspoon, rinse and pat dry, season with salt and pepper, brush with Garlic Butter [see recipe 8] and place under pre-heated grill. Cooking time depends on the size of the crayfish, anything from 15–30 minutes.

Before serving, brush with a little more garlic butter, or serve sauce separately.

Serve with a salad and crispy hot Garlic or Herb Bread [34, 35].

*Note:* When grilling frozen Rock Lobster, defrost, then dip in boiling water for just one minute. This will ensure a perfect dish.

# 109. Sherry-grilled Crayfish

Follow instructions for Grilled Crayfish [108], and baste flesh with 6 Tblsp melted butter into which have been mixed 3 Tblsp dry sherry, ½ tsp paprika and a pinch of cayenne pepper.

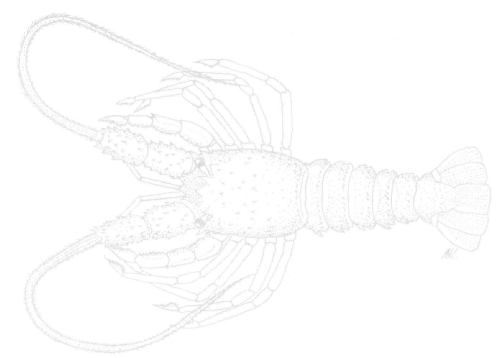

# 110. Barbecued Crayfish

Prepare as for Grilled Crayfish [108], then place flesh-down over medium coals for 1½ minutes. Turn over, baste liberally with melted butter and grill for 15–20 minutes more.

# 111. Sultan's Crayfish

The flesh of four raw or cooked Rock
    Lobsters, including the legs, or
    equivalent amount in fresh tail meat,
    diced
3 Tblsp butter
2 onions, sliced
2 cloves garlic, crushed
2 tomatoes, skinned and chopped
1 tsp cumin
1 tsp coriander
2 tsp turmeric
¼ tsp chilli powder
2 cups milk
1 tsp garam-masala
1½ tsp salt
  squeeze of lemon juice
2 Tblsp chopped parsley

*An aromatic curry using subtly-blended spices to complement the delicious flavour of crayfish.*

Sauté onions and garlic in butter until brown. Add tomatoes, spices, (excluding garam-masala), and milk. Cook, uncovered, until stock reduces and the sauce thickens – about 30–45 minutes.

Add crayfish, salt and garam-masala. Heat thoroughly or – if you're using diced fresh meat – cook through. Add a squeeze of lemon juice and some chopped parsley.

Serve with Chipattis, [39], chopped bananas dredged in desiccated coconut, and a salad of finely chopped tomatoes green peppers and spring onions.

Serves four.

# 112. Sultan's Entrée

See plate 8

*Sultan's Crayfish [111] is so special that everyone licks their platters clean so it's most unlikely you'll have any left over with which to make this dish.*

Make a half quantity of Sultan's Crayfish, let it cool while you cut four avocado pears in half. Sprinkle each half with a little lemon juice and salt, cut a sliver of skin off the underside and stand each half on a side plate.

Spoon Sultan's Crayfish into each avocado pear half, decorate with a sprig of fresh parsley and serve with crisp apple wedges.

Serves eight.

# 113. Crayfish Cocktail

Dice the flesh of one large or two small cooked rock lobsters. Mix with Seafood Sauce [7].

Serve on a bed of lettuce, garnished with a sprig of parsley and a lemon wedge.

Serves four.

# 114. Avocado Ritz

Into avocado pear halves, which you've liberally sprinkled with salt and lemon juice, spoon Crayfish Cocktail [113]. Garnish as above and serve with tomato wedges on a crisp lettuce leaf.

# 115. Lobster Melon Cocktail

Spoon Crayfish Cocktail [113] into spaanspek halves. Garnish with a sprig of parsley and a lemon wedge.

Ring the changes by mixing the lobster with any of the Seafood Sauce Variations [7].

ALTERNATIVES:
Cooked, diced Monkfish, Prawns, Shrimps. Smoked, flaked fish or smoked, chopped Oysters or Mussels.

# 116. Caribbean Paella

6 Tblsp olive oil
1 kg Chicken (6 thighs) cubed and de-boned
1 Rock Lobster, uncooked, cubed
300 g Prawns, uncooked, in or out of their shells
300 g cubed ham
300 g prepared Mussels, steamed and removed from their shells (about 35)
2 medium-sized onions, sliced
2 ripe tomatoes, skinned and chopped
2 green peppers, sliced
2 cloves garlic, crushed
1½ cups uncooked rice
2½ cups chicken stock
250 g cooked peas
1 tsp turmeric
   salt and freshly-ground black pepper

*A very special dish for easy entertaining, which can be made in advance.*

Heat half the oil in a heavy-bottomed frying pan and brown chicken, a few pieces at a time. Season with salt and pepper and set aside. Cook lobster and prawns in the pan and set aside separately from the chicken.

Add remaining olive oil and sauté onion and garlic until golden. Add green peppers, tomatoes and half the stock. Return chicken to pan and cook gently for 15 minutes.

Add ham, rice, turmeric, remaining stock and a little more salt and pepper and simmer until rice is cooked.

Return lobster and prawns to the Paella and lastly the mussels and peas. Stir Paella very gently and heat through. A dash of dry white wine may be used to moisten the dish, if necessary. Check seasoning.

Serve with hot crispy Herb Bread [34] and a tossed French Salad [36].

Serves six.

# 117. Shellfish Salad

See plate 9

On a bed of shredded lettuce arrange diced, cooked lobster flesh, whole peeled prawns, diced crab meat, prepared mussels and periwinkles.

Garnish with tomato wedges, anchovy fillets, capers, olives, spring onions, quartered hard-boiled eggs and sprinkle with chopped parsley and chervil.

Alternatively arrange ingredients in a deep salad bowl as illustrated in the photograph.

Season with salt and freshly-ground black pepper and, just before serving, sprinkle with French Dressing [9].

# 118. Aegean Island Pâté

198 g tin Cod's Roe, or fresh Fish Roe
5 slices white bread, minus crusts
2 level tsp grated onion
1 clove garlic, crushed
6 Tblsp olive oil
6 Tblsp cream
1 Tblsp gelatine
2½ Tblsp lemon juice
4 anchovies (2 tsp), pounded
1 Tblsp tomato sauce
   salt and freshly-ground black pepper

Dissolve gelatine in lemon juice in a pan of hot water. Emulsify olive oil and cream, pour over bread and blend well. Add onion, garlic, salt, pepper, tomato sauce, roe and anchovy, mix well and finally add gelatine and lemon juice.

Sieve finely or blend in a liquidiser.

Chill and garnish with a sprig of parsley. Serve with black olives, or on biscuits with pre-dinner drinks.

# 119. Poached Roe Mornay

500 g Fish Roe
Mornay Sauce [10]
Grated Parmesan cheese

Poach roe for 10 minutes in water and 1 tsp vinegar. Cool, remove skin and cut into small pieces. Combine with Mornay Sauce, mixing carefully so as not to pulverise the roe.

Butter 4 scallop shells, spoon in Roe mixture, sprinkle generously with Parmesan cheese and bake for 8–10 minutes at 190°C until heated through and the topping is crisp.

Serve with Palm Bread [33].

Serves four.

# 120. Mock Caviare

250 g Fish Roe, poached for 10 minutes
   in water and 1 tsp lemon juice
½ tsp salt
   freshly-ground black pepper
1 tsp grated onion
1 Tblsp brandy
   squeeze of lemon juice

*Cross the costly roe of the virgin Sturgeon off your shopping list – here's the perfect substitute for this Imperial tit-bit.*

Split roe, remove skin and crumble in a small bowl. Add salt, pepper, grated onion, brandy and lemon juice and mix lightly with a fork.

Serve with lemon wedges, garnished with a sprig of parsley on rye bread or biscuits for hors d'oeuvres and snacks and you'll not call the Empress Catherine your great-aunt!

Mock Caviare improves with keeping – store in your fridge for 2–3 weeks with confidence.

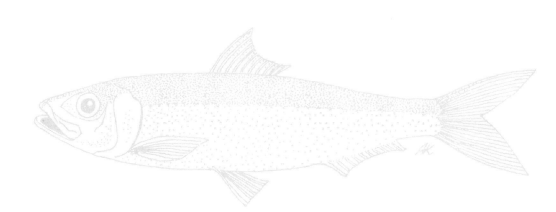

# 121. Savoy Sardines

12 Sardines
  salt
½ cup finely chopped spring onions
5 Tblsp dry white wine
2 Tblsp water
1 Tblsp lemon juice
  butter
  chopped parsley

Wash and dry whole sardines. Season to taste with salt, then lay in a buttered baking dish which has been sprinkled with chopped spring onions. Pour over wine, water and lemon juice, dot with butter and bake at 180°C for 8–10 minutes.

Sprinkle with chopped parsley and serve as an hors d'oeuvre.

Serves four.

# 122. Sardine Butter

75 g Sardine fillets
1 tsp olive oil
½ cup soft butter
  salt and freshly-ground black pepper

Pound sardine fillets in oil. Blend in butter, season to taste with salt and pepper and serve on crisp fried triangles of bread, garnished with sprigs of parsley.

# 123. Scallops with Garlic Butter

750 g Scallops, cleaned and sliced
  salt and white pepper
  flour
2 Tblsp butter
2 Tblsp oil
  Garlic Butter, [8]
  chopped parsley and lemon wedges

Season scallop slices with salt and pepper and dip in flour. Fry in hot butter and oil until lightly browned. Do this in batches so as not to overcrowd pan.

Transfer to a heated serving dish, garnish with a little chopped parsley and serve with lemon wedges and hot garlic butter.

Serves four to six.

# 124. Coquilles Saint-Jacques à la Parisienne

Court Bouillon, [1] to which add ½ chicken stock cube
1 kg Scallops cut into 2 cm slices
2 cups (350 g) sliced mushrooms
Cheese Sauce Parisienne, [18]
Creamy mashed potato for piping round scallop shells
Grated Parmesan cheese

In a medium saucepan, simmer scallops and mushrooms in court bouillon, covered, for 4–5 minutes. Drain, then mix into two thirds of the Sauce Parisienne, stirring gently.

Butter six scallop shells, pipe mashed potatoes round the edges, fill with scallop mixture, mask with the remaining sauce and sprinkle with Parmesan cheese. Bake at 180°C for 10–15 minutes and brown the top quickly under the grill.

Serves six.

ALTERNATIVE:

Mussels may be used in place of scallops to make a more economical dish. In this case they are best cut in half and added to the recipe when the simmered mushrooms are mixed with Sauce Parisienne.

# 125. Boiled Sea Urchins

Cook sea urchins for 4–5 minutes in boiling salted water then drain and cut open with a pair of scissors on the concave side, where the mouth is situated. Drain well and discard the dark excremental part then dip buttered fingers of bread into the shell.

Wash down with plenty of cold white wine.

# 126. Seaweed Jelly

*Here's a recipe for a little-known delicacy – a delicious jelly made from the delicate light brown seaweed fronds which cling to the long stalks of sea bamboo.*

Collect a handful of seaweed and boil in water for 3 hours. When strained and set, it becomes a pure, healthful and beautifully-textured jelly which one may flavour with sugar, cinnamon, fruit juices, vanilla etc.

The jelly can also be used as aspic and all manner of goodies such as left-over flaked fish, peas, beetroot or chicken may be set in its fragrant depths.

Incidentally, seaweed jelly and lemon is one of the remedies used by fishermen along our coast for coughs and colds.

# 127. French Skate

1 kg Skate wings, washed and dried
4 medium-sized onions, sliced
2 cloves garlic, chopped
3 Tblsp butter
2 Tblsp flour
2 cups milk
½ chicken stock cube, crumbled
1 bay leaf
  pinch thyme
½ tsp salt
  freshly-ground black pepper
4 Tblsp grated Grùyere cheese

Sauté onions and garlic in butter until tender. Remove from heat, mix in stock cube and flour, then slowly add milk. Simmer, stirring, until thick and creamy. Add seasoning and 2 Tblsp cheese and poach skate wings in this sauce for 10–15 minutes until cooked.

Transfer to a heated ovenproof serving dish, sprinkle with remaining cheese and bake in a hot oven until topping is golden.

Serve with boiled new potatoes tossed in butter.

Serves six.

ALTERNATIVES:

Shark, Hottentot

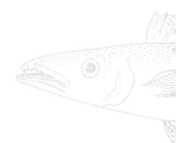

# 128. Mustard Cream Skate

4 slices skinned Skate wings
250 ml cream, beaten thick
4 Tblsp hot mustard
   salt and freshly-ground black pepper

*This recipe is so delicious and simple, that it should encourage anyone who hasn't tried skate to do so at once !*

Rinse and dry skate wings. Season with salt and pepper and spread on either side with mustard. Place in a baking dish, pour over the cream and bake, covered, for 20 minutes at 180°C until fish is cooked.

Serve with boiled new potatoes, tossed in butter, and a Green Salad [36].

Serves four.

ALTERNATIVE:

Shark

# 129. Skate with Black Butter

1 kg Skate wings
   Court Bouillon [1], to which add
      1 Tblsp wine vinegar
2 Tblsp chopped parsley

**BLACK BUTTER SAUCE**

4 Tblsp butter
3 tsp chopped capers
2 Tblsp white vinegar

*An interesting combination of flavours: the delicate flavour of Skate and a buttery sauce sharpened with capers and vinegar.*

Wash skate wings, cut into serving portions and poach in court bouillon for 10–15 minutes. Place on a board and lift flesh from bones. Transfer fish to a warmed serving dish, sprinkle with chopped parsley and keep warm.

Make sauce by browning butter in a small saucepan, being careful not to let it burn. Remove from heat, stir in capers and vinegar, pour over fish and serve at once.

Serves six.

ALTERNATIVES:

Shark, Sole.

# 130. Simmered Snoek

*Unimaginative, we hear you snort, making as if to turn over the page. It isn't! It's marvellous and the only way, our gaffers say, a true South African fisherman will eat it.*

Clean snoek, 'vlek' by cutting down next to backbone so that it hinges at the stomach. Sprinkle liberally with salt and wind-dry for 8 hours.

Cut into smaller pieces, place in a large saucepan and cover with salted water. Bring to the boil, then simmer gently for about 10 minutes until fish is cooked.

Drain and serve with new potatoes tossed in parsley butter, or flake the fish and serve on open sandwiches with chutney.

# 131. Smoked Snoek Quiche

**25 cm Pie Plate lined with Quiche Pastry [3], baked blind.**

**FILLING**

**2 Tblsp butter**
**2 Tblsp flour**
**¼ tsp salt**
   **freshly-ground black pepper**
   **pinch cayenne pepper**
**1 cup milk**
**1 cup cream**
**3 eggs, lightly beaten**
**2 Tblsp grated Cheddar cheese**
**2 Tblsp finely-chopped parsley**
**1½ cups flaked, smoked Snoek**
**2 Tblsp toasted crumbs**
**2 Tblsp grated Parmesan cheese**

Melt butter in small saucepan. Remove from heat, stir in flour, seasoning and milk. Return to heat and cook, stirring, until sauce becomes smooth and thick.

Mix cream and eggs together, add Cheddar cheese, parsley and flaked snoek. Add to white sauce, then spoon filling into pastry case. Sprinkle with mixed toasted crumbs and Parmesan cheese and bake for 30 minutes at 180°C until filling has set and topping is crunchy and golden.

Serves six.

*Note:* Any smoked fish may be used in this recipe.

# 132. Smoorvis

500 g Smoked Snoek, flaked and de-boned
2 onions, sliced
2 Tblsp oil
2 Tblsp butter
2 potatoes, peeled and cut into tiny dice
2 large tomatoes, peeled and chopped
2 chillies, pounded or finely chopped,
    or 1 tsp chilli powder
    freshly-ground black pepper
2 cups cooked rice
5 Tblsp sultanas (optional)
    squeeze of lemon
    chopped parsley

*This delicious dish is traditionally made with smoked snoek but any dry, smoked fish could be used.*

Heat the oil and butter in a large, heavy saucepan and sauté onions until golden brown. Add potatoes, tomatoes, chillies, pepper and cook for a little longer until the potatoes start to brown. Add fish, rice and sultanas, cover and cook over a low heat until potatoes are just cooked through.

Before serving, stir in a squeeze of lemon juice and sprinkle with chopped parsley.

Smoorvis is traditionally served with black grape jam or fruit atjar and home-made brown bread.

Serves six not-too-hungry people.

# 133. Smoked Snoek Pâté

200 g Smoked Snoek, flaked
150 g butter
1 medium-sized onion, chopped
    juice of ½ lemon
    freshly-ground black pepper
125 ml cream
4 drops red cochineal

Sauté onions in half the butter until soft and transparent. Remove from heat, add remaining butter, flaked fish, lemon juice, plenty of pepper, cream and cochineal. Mix well.

Blend in a liquidiser, check seasoning and refrigerate.

Spread reverently and abundantly on Palm Bread [33].

# 134. Quick Snoek Liver Pâté

250 g Snoek livers
2 Tblsp butter
    juice of ½ lemon
¼ cup dry white wine
¼ cup water
6 Tblsp cream
¼ tsp Worcestershire sauce
    pinch cayenne pepper
    salt and freshly-ground black pepper

*Salvage fresh snoek livers to make this flavoursome spread for brown bread or biscuits.*

Sauté livers in butter for a minute or two. Add lemon juice, wine, water, Worcestershire sauce and seasoning. Simmer, uncovered, for five minutes, remove from heat and add cream. Blend in a liquidiser and refrigerate until required.

# 135. Crumbed Snoek Livers

Snoek livers – most gourmets turn up their noses at them – are delicious. Simply marinate in salt, pepper and lemon juice, then roll in breadcrumbs and fry in butter. Garnish with a sprinkling of nutmeg.

# 136. Sole Véronique

500 g Sole fillets, rolled up and
    secured with toothpicks
2 Tblsp butter
1½ cups sliced mushrooms
½ cup dry white wine
¼ cup Fish Stock, [2]
125 ml cream
2 egg yolks
200 g white grapes, peeled and de-pipped
    (using the closed end of a hair clip)
    salt and white pepper

Season fish with salt and pepper.

Sauté mushrooms in butter until soft. Add fish, pour over wine and stock, cover and poach slowly for 10–15 minutes, until fish is cooked through.

Remove fish to heated serving platter and keep warm.

Strain sauce into a small saucepan. Mix egg yolks and cream, add to sauce and cook, stirring continuously over a low heat until sauce thickens. Add grapes and heat through.

Pour sauce over fish and serve at once with fluffy mashed potatoes.

Serves four.

ALTERNATIVES:

Kingklip, Barbel, Gurnard, Monkfish

# 137. Coconut Bay Sole

See plate 8

4 Soles, skinned and trimmed
    lemon juice
    salt and white pepper
2 beaten eggs
¼ cup toasted crumbs
¼ cup desiccated coconut
    butter and oil for frying
4 bananas

Season soles with a little lemon juice, salt and pepper. Dip in egg, then coat with breadcrumbs and coconut, mixed. Fry in hot butter and oil until golden, being careful not to let butter burn. Drain and place on warmed serving platter.

Cut bananas in half, sprinkle with lemon juice and fry gently in pan in which sole was cooked, adding more butter if necessary. Place two halves on each sole, and serve at once.

Serves four lovers of coconut.

ALTERNATIVES:

Gurnard, Kingklip, Monkfish.

# 138. Crumbed Calamari with Tartare Sauce

500 g Squid, cleaned and dried
2 eggs, lightly beaten
    toasted breadcrumbs
    salt and freshly-ground black pepper
    oil for deep frying
    Tartare Sauce, [13]

Cut squid into rings, steam for five minutes, season with salt and pepper and dip in egg and toasted crumbs. Deep fry in hot oil until crispy golden-brown (about two minutes). Do this in batches so as not to overcrowd the pan.

Scrumptious with Tartare Sauce and Persian Rice, [38]. Serves four.

*Note:* Make a meal of mixed seafood deep fried in this way – Prawns, Cubed Lobster, Scallops etc.

117

# 139. Portuguese Stuffed Squid

8 15 cm whole squid or 6 larger ones
2 Tblsp butter
2 Tblsp oil
2 cloves garlic, roughly chopped
  seasoned flour for dredging

STUFFING
5 Tblsp butter
1 medium-sized onion, chopped
2 cloves garlic, chopped
2 medium-sized ripe tomatoes, peeled
  and chopped
1 small green pepper, chopped
$\frac{1}{4}$ tsp oregano
2 tsp salt
  freshly-ground black pepper
$\frac{1}{2}$ cup uncooked rice
$\frac{1}{2}$ cup dry white wine
$\frac{1}{2}$ cup water

Clean squid, following directions on p. 53. Dry cones, fins and tentacles and set aside.

Make stuffing: Brown onions in butter, add garlic, tomatoes, green pepper and seasoning. Mix well and simmer for a minute or two. Stir in rice, wine and water, cover and simmer slowly until all the liquid has been absorbed and the rice is cooked.

In another saucepan heat the oil and butter and fry roughly-chopped garlic for a few minutes, being careful not to let it burn. Remove garlic from the pan and discard. Finely chop fins and tentacles and brown in the same oil. Add to stuffing, mixing well.

Lightly season inside squid cones, add stuffing but don't pack too tightly as squid shrinks when cooking. Secure open ends with skewers or toothpicks. Dredge with seasoned flour and brown very well in the garlicky oil.

Reduce heat, cover and simmer very slowly for about 1 hour until squid is tender.

Serve with a Green Salad [36].

Serves four.

# 140. Milanese Fish Pie

500 g cooked, flaked Stockfish, or
  other cooked fish
1 kg potatoes, boiled and mashed with
  seasoning, a little milk and a small,
  finely-chopped onion
2 hard boiled eggs, chopped
1 Tblsp parsley
2 Tblsp chopped chives or spring onions
  salt and freshly-ground black pepper
  a dash of Worcestershire sauce
2 skinned, chopped tomatoes
  Cheese Sauce, [19]
  toasted breadcrumbs

Line a casserole dish with half the mashed potatoes.

Mix fish, hard-boiled eggs, parsley, chives, tomatoes, seasoning and Worcestershire sauce. Combine fish mixture with Simple Cheese Sauce and fill the potato-lined casserole. Cover with remaining mashed potatoes, sprinkle with toasted crumbs and bake at 180°C for 20 minutes.

Serve with a French Salad [36].

Serves 4–6.

# 141. Mediterranean Stuffed Tomatoes

6 large, firm, ripe tomatoes
1 cup flaked Smoked Haddock
2 medium-sized ripe tomatoes, peeled,
    seeded and chopped
2 Tblsp finely-chopped anchovies
12 stoned, finely-chopped black olives
1 clove garlic, crushed
4 Tblsp dry breadcrumbs
2 Tblsp olive oil
    salt and freshly-ground black pepper

Cut the stalk end off 6 tomatoes and carefully remove the pith with a sharpened teaspoon. Sprinkle cavities with a little salt and set aside, open end down, on kitchen paper. Reserve pith.

Mix fish, anchovies, chopped tomatoes, reserved pith, olives, garlic, breadcrumbs and oil. Season with a little salt and plenty of pepper.

Spoon stuffing into tomatoes, replacing each 'lid' and place on a greased baking tray. Bake for 20 minutes at 150°C.

Serve hot or cold.

Serves six.

# 142. Nordic Fish Loaf

1 Tblsp butter
2 Tblsp toasted breadcrumbs
700 g Stockfish, skinned, de-boned and
    cut into small cubes
250 ml cream
8 Tblsp milk
1 Tblsp cornflour
1 tsp salt
½ tsp white pepper
    twists of lemon and sprigs of parsley
    for garnishing

*This simple and classical dish allows the flavour of the fish to come shining through. It can be served cold with salads or hot with a complementary sauce.*

Grease a small loaf tin with butter, sprinkle with crumbs, shaking tin gently to ensure even distribution. Turn tin upside down to shake off excess. Crumbs that is!

Slake cornflour in milk. Pour cream into electric blender, add fish piece by piece – no quicker, or it will be difficult to blend. Add seasoning and milk and cornflour mixture. Blend until you have a smooth purée.

Pour into loaf tin and bake in a bain-marie for 1–1¼ hours at 160°C, being careful not to allow the water to boil. To test if loaf is cooked, insert a skewer. If it comes out clean, turn loaf out onto a serving platter and decorate with twists of lemon and sprigs of parsley.

Serving your Nordic Loaf hot? Let it go hand in hand with one of the following sauces: Spicy Tomato Sauce [11], Mushroom Sauce [12], Mornay Sauce [10], to which add chopped shrimps.

Serves 4–5 as a main course or 6–8 as an hors d'oeuvre.

ALTERNATIVES:

Gurnard, Kabeljou, Kingklip, Monkfish, Musselcracker, Silver Fish.

# 143. Hake Soufflé

**500 g Fillets of Hake**
**2 cups milk**
**1½ Tblsp butter**
**2 Tblsp flour**
**3 eggs, separated**
**½ tsp salt**
  **freshly-ground black pepper**
**¼ tsp dry mustard**

Poach fish in milk, seasoned with salt and pepper. When cooked, cool and flake, removing skin and bones.

Make a white sauce by melting butter in a small saucepan. Remove from heat, stir in flour and 2 cups milk in which fish has been poached. Return to heat and cook, stirring continuously, until sauce is smooth and thickened. Stir in beaten egg yolks and mustard.

Add flaked fish to sauce, then fold in whipped egg whites carefully, until no streaks are left.

Pour into buttered soufflé or casserole dish and bake at 150°C for 30 minutes.

Serve with a salad of tomatoes, cucumbers and chopped spring onions.

Serves four.

ALTERNATIVES:

Angel Fish, Cape Salmon, Gurnard, Kabeljou, Kingklip, Monkfish, Musselcracker, Rock Cod, Silverfish, Yellowtail, or any leftover fish.

# 144. Fish Cakes

**500 g steamed Stockfish (or other left-**
  **over cooked fish)**
**300 g potatoes, boiled and mashed**
  **without milk or butter**
**4 Tblsp grated onion**
**3 Tblsp chopped parsley**
**1 tsp salt**
  **freshly-ground black pepper to taste**
  **pinch nutmeg**
**2 eggs**
  **toasted crumbs**

Remove skin and bones from fish, flake and combine with mashed potatoes, onion, parsley, salt, pepper, nutmeg and eggs. Mix well.

Place crumbs in a small round bowl. Using a soup spoon, drop fish cake mixture in and rotate bowl to coat evenly with crumbs. Flatten cakes slightly, set aside and continue until all the mixture has been used up.

Fry fish cakes in hot oil, drain on kitchen paper and serve with lemon wedges, or a complementary sauce.

Makes about 16 fish cakes.

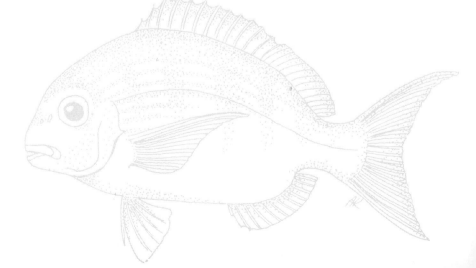

# 145. Wine-baked Stumpnose

1,5 kg White or Red Stumpnose
  Tangy Bacon and Mushroom Stuffing,
  [27]
½ cup dry white wine
¼ cup water
½ chicken stock cube
1 cup cream – fresh or sour
1 tsp cornflour
4 shallots or spring onions
2 Tblsp chopped parsley
  mashed potatoes

*An excellent recipe for most fish which can be baked whole. It's essential though, that they are of suitable size: not less than 750 g or larger than 2 kg.*

Stuff fish, sew up with strong thread and place in a large baking dish. Pour wine and water over fish, cover dish and bake at 180°C for about 45 minutes until cooked, removing cover for the final 10 minutes to crisp the skin slightly. Transfer to a warmed serving platter,

Place baking dish on top of stove over medium heat and gradually stir in combined stock cube, cream and cornflour. Mix well, then add shallots and parsley. Simmer gently until shallots are tender, transfer sauce to a gravy boat and keep warm.

Pipe fluffy mashed potatoes round the edge of serving dish and sprinkle fish and potatoes with a little chopped parsley.

## TO SERVE

Cut off stitches, remove fins carefully and slip a fish server (or egg flip) between side fillet and backbone. Lift fillet off in one piece. Turn fish over and lift off second fillet.

## ALTERNATIVES

Suitable sized Roman, Red Steenbras, Angel Fish, Baardman, Cape Salmon, Galjoen, Kabeljou, Musselcracker, Silver Fish.

# 146. Barbados Tuna

1 kg Tuna, cut into large cubes
  juice of one large lemon
¼ cup dry white wine
¼ cup chicken stock
2 large onions, finely sliced
1 clove garlic, crushed
1 green pepper, finely sliced
6 bananas, peeled and sliced
2 Tblsp butter
5 Tblsp oil
4 cloves
1 bay leaf
¼ tsp thyme
  salt and freshly-ground black pepper
  flour

Season tuna with salt and pepper and marinate in lemon juice, wine and chicken stock for 30 minutes. Drain fish, reserving the marinade, sprinkle lightly with flour and brown quickly in oil and butter. Remove from saucepan and set aside.

Brown onions and garlic in the same saucepan, scraping up all the brown bits from the pan. Add green pepper, bananas, cloves, bay leaf, thyme and marinade, season with salt and pepper. Cover and simmer gently for 15 minutes.

Return fish to saucepan, cover and simmer for a further 20 minutes.

Serve with fluffy mashed potatoes

Serves six.

## ALTERNATIVES

Marlin, Cape Salmon, Angel Fish, Leervis, Yellowtail.

# 147. Apple-braised Tuna with Cherries

500 g cooking apples
6 Tblsp butter
1 kg Tuna, cut into steaks
2 lemons
250 g cherries, pitted
¼ cup dry white wine
¼ cup chicken stock
  cinnamon
  salt and freshly-ground black pepper

Reserve 2 apples. Peel and core the rest and cut into wedges.

In a heavy saucepan melt half the butter and sauté tuna steaks lightly on both sides. Season well with salt and pepper. Add apple wedges and the juice of one lemon. Cover and cook gently for 10 minutes. Add cherries, wine, stock and a little cinnamon and cook for a further 20 minutes.

Sauté remaining apple wedges in the rest of the butter until nicely browned, but not too soft.

Place tuna steaks on a heated serving platter. Correct the sauce for seasoning, then pour it over the tuna and garnish with apple and lemon wedges.

Serve with fluffy mashed potatoes.

Serves six.

ALTERNATIVE
Marlin.

# 148. Roast Tuna Spiked with Bacon

Prepare whole tuna or section of tuna for roasting. Wash well, remove skin, pat dry and make incisions in the flesh with the tip of a vegetable knife. Into each incision place a sliver of streaky bacon.

Season fish with salt and freshly-ground black pepper, then wrap more slices of bacon round the outside of the fish, securing the ends with toothpicks.

Heat 1 cm of oil in roasting pan and brown bacon-wrapped fish all over. Reduce the heat to 160°C–170°C and roast, covered, for approximately 35 minutes per kilo, basting frequently with hot oil.

Serve with a Green Salad [36].

# 149. Tuna and Mushroom Casserole

4 cups cooked rice
200 g cooked, flaked tuna, or substitute tinned light-meat tuna
1 small onion, grated
440 g can mushroom soup
½ Tblsp mustard
  salt and freshly-ground black pepper
1 cup grated Cheddar cheese
  tomato wedges and fresh, sliced mush-
    rooms for garnishing

Combine all ingredients in a buttered, ovenproof dish, using only half the cheese. Mix well.

Sprinkle the remaining cheese on top and bake at 180°C for about 20 minutes, until the topping is crispy brown.

Garnish with tomato wedges and sliced mushrooms and serve with a Green Salad [36].

Serves six.

# 150. Macaroni and Tuna Bake

200 g Macaroni, cooked and rinsed
400 g cooked, flaked tuna, fresh or
    tinned
Cheese Sauce [19], to which add extra
    tsp mustard, 1 Tblsp Worcestershire
    Sauce and ½ cup medium dry sherry
Parmesan Cheese, for topping.

Mix all ingredients together in a buttered, ovenproof baking dish. Top with Parmesan cheese and bake at 180°C for about 20 minutes until the top has browned.

Serve with Hot Herb or Garlic Bread [recipes 35 and 34] and a Green Salad [36].

Serves six.

ALTERNATIVE:

Yellowtail, freshly-cooked or tinned.

# 151. Salade Niçoise

200 g Tuna, canned or freshly poached,
    drained and flaked.
6 Anchovy Fillets, soaked for 2 hrs in
    warm milk
3 tomatoes, cut in wedges
250 g french green beans, cooked, drain-
    ed, then refreshed under cold running
    water to bring back the colour
  black olives, de-pipped
½ cucumber, peeled and sliced into rings
1 small green pepper, cut into rings
1 lettuce heart, fresh and crisp, and
    torn into pieces
  chopped parsley
  French dressing, [9]

In an oval serving dish arrange the salad; placing lettuce at the bottom, then the beans and tuna flakes. Line the rim of the dish with cucumber and decorate the salad with green pepper, tomato wedges, olives and anchovy fillets in a criss cross design. Sprinkle chopped parsley over the top and add french dressing just before serving.

Serves six as an hors d'oeuvre.

# 152. Foil-baked Tuna

Cut tuna steaks into individual portions, season with plenty of salt and freshly-ground black pepper.

Butter pieces of aluminium foil, using plenty of butter and sprinkle freshly-chopped parsley and dry basil thereon. Place tuna steaks in the middle, add a squeeze of lemon juice, seal and bake for 20–30 minutes until fish flakes easily.

Serve with the herb-butter from the foil.

# 153. Bacon-wrapped Tuna

Follow recipe for Foil-baked Tuna [152], but wrap each tuna steak in streaky bacon. Open foil during final 5 minutes of the cooking process to crisp bacon.

# 154. Bacon and Banana-wrapped Tuna

Follow recipe for Foil-baked Tuna [152] but place bacon slices on a chopping board, cover bacon with mashed banana, place Tuna steaks in the middle and wrap up before placing in foil. Open foil during final 5 minutes to crisp bacon.

NOTE

Any of the above three recipes may be successfully transferred to your barbecue.

ALTERNATIVES

Marlin, Angel Fish.

# 155. Mandarin Tuna Salad

200 g tin light-meat tuna, drained and
    flaked
1 small lettuce, clean and crisp
1 small tin mandarin oranges,
    drained
1 apple, cut in fine wedges and
    sprinkled with lemon juice
50 g toasted, flaked almonds
1 Tblsp chopped parsley
    Seafood Sauce, [7], or one of the
    Seafood Sauce Variations.

Line a serving platter with lettuce torn into small pieces.

Gently toss tuna, apple wedges and mandarin orange segments in sauce, reserving some for decoration. Distribute tuna mixture over lettuce, decorate with reserved apple wedges and mandarin orange segments, sprinkle with almonds and parsley.

Serves four.

# 156. Braised Bonito

6 Bonito Steaks 3 cm thick, dipped in
    seasoned flour
3 Tblsp butter
3 Tblsp oil
1 medium-sized onion, sliced
2 medium-sized ripe tomatoes, peeled
    and sliced
1 cup chopped mushrooms
¼ cup dry red wine
½ beef stock cube dissolved in ¼ cup hot
    water
    salt and freshly-ground black pepper

Brown bonito steaks in butter and oil, remove from frying pan and season with plenty of freshly-ground black pepper and a little salt.

Brown onions in the same pan, then add tomatoes, mushrooms and black pepper and simmer, covered, for ten minutes. Mix wine and stock into onion mixture, then return fish to pan. Cover with spoonfuls of onion mixture and simmer, uncovered, for a further 10–15 minutes until fish is cooked through.

Serve with boiled potatoes tossed in parsley butter.

Serves six.

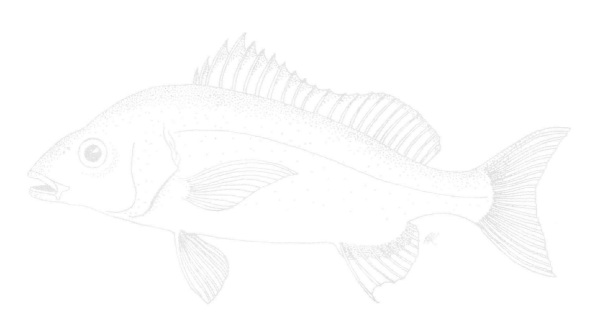

# 157. Herb-grilled White Steenbras

4 whole White Steenbras, about 350 g
    each, cleaned and prepared for
    grilling.
  oil
  salt and freshly-ground black pepper
1 onion, thinly sliced
4 rashers bacon, cut in small pieces
2 cloves garlic, chopped fine
  dried sage
  dried thyme
  oil and lemon juice for basting

Brush fish inside and out with oil, season with salt and pepper. Sprinkle stomach cavity with a pinch each of sage and thyme, stuff with onion rings, bacon and a little chopped garlic.

Sew up fish and grill in the oven or over medium coals, in a hinged grid, for about 10 minutes on each side, or until flesh flakes easily with a fork. Baste with oil and lemon juice while cooking.

Serves four.

### ALTERNATIVES

John Dory, Blacktail, Bream, Dageraad, Grunter, Roman, Silver Fish, Blue Hottentot, Elf, Red Steenbras, Jacobever.

# 158. Quick Yellowtail Loaf

400 g freshly cooked yellowtail (or sub-
    stitute 2 x 200 g tins yellowtail,
    drained)
3 eggs, lightly beaten
1 cup milk, or milk and cream
2 Tblsp chopped chives
2 Tblsp chopped spring onions
2 Tblsp lemon juice
½ tsp Worcestershire sauce
  salt and white pepper to taste

Flake fish finely, removing skin and bones. Mix together with remaining ingredients, pour into a small, greased loaf tin and bake at 180°C for 30 minutes.

Turn out and serve hot, with a complementary sauce, or cold with salads.

Serves six.

### ALTERNATIVES

Cape Salmon, Kabeljou, Snoek.

# 159. Ouma's Pickled Fish

1,7 kg Yellowtail, cleaned, filleted and
    cut into slices
  oil
6 bay leaves
6 large onions, sliced into rings
3 cups brown vinegar
1 cup water
¾ cup sugar
1 Tblsp turmeric
3 Tblsp curry powder
2 rounded Tblsp flour
1½ tsp salt
1 Tblsp black peppercorns
  freshly-ground black pepper
1 cup sultanas (optional)

Fry fish cubes in oil for about 1½ minutes on each side until just cooked through. Season well with salt and pepper and set aside.

Simmer onions in vinegar, water, bay leaves, sugar, turmeric, curry powder, salt and peppercorns for 10–12 minutes until they are just cooked, but still crisp. Thicken the sauce with flour mixed to a smooth paste with a little of the hot sauce.

Place layers of fish, onions and sultanas in an airtight container. Pour sauce over and refrigerate.

After 3 days, the fish will be ready to eat, and it will keep for six months.

## ALTERNATIVES

Cape Salmon, Kabeljou, Musselcraker, Leervis, Mackerel, Snoek, Spanish Mackerel.

# Seafood Index

127

# Recipe Index

130

131

133